Spies Beneath Berlin

By the same author

From Anarchism to Reformism
Britain and European Resistance 1940–1945
Camp X
The Silent Game
Spy Wars
Churchill and Secret Service
Roosevelt and Churchill
Secret Agent: The True Story of the Covert War Against Hitler

American–British–Canadian Intelligence Relations, 1939–2000
(edited with Rhodri Jeffreys-Jones)

SPIES
BENEATH
BERLIN

DAVID STAFFORD

THE OVERLOOK PRESS
Woodstock & New York

First published in the United States in 2003 by
The Overlook Press, Peter Mayer Publishers, Inc.
Woodstock & New York

WOODSTOCK:
One Overlook Drive
Woodstock, NY 12498
www.overlookpress.com
[for individual orders, bulk and special sales, contact our Woodstock office]

NEW YORK:
141 Wooster Street
New York, NY 10012

⊚ The paper used in this book meets the requirements for paper
permanence as described in the ANSI Z39.48-1992 standard.

Library of Congress Cataloging-in-Publication Data

Stafford, David.
Spies beneath Berlin / David Stafford.
p. cm.
Includes bibliographical references and index.
1. Operation Stopwatch/Gold, Berlin, Germany, 1955-1956.
2. United States. Central Intelligence Agency. 3. Great Britain. Secret Intelligence
Service. 4. Soviet Union. Komitet gosudarstvennoæ
bezopasnosti. 5. Berlin (Germany)—History—1945-1990.
6. Electronic intelligence—Germany—Berlin. 7. Cold War. I. Title
UB271.U5 S73 2003   327.1273043'1552'09045—dc21   2002034628

Printed in the United States of America
ISBN 1-58567-361-7
FIRST EDITION
1 3 5 7 9 8 6 4 2

For my sister Liz, fellow survivor
of the Cold War

Contents

Contents

Acknowledgements

I first thought of writing this book in June 1999, during a walk along the shore of the Starnberger See at Tutzing, outside Munich, during a conference on Germany and Cold War intelligence. My old friend Bill Leary, professor of history at the University of Georgia, gave a brief paper on this legendary operation. German scholars attending the conference were aware of the Berlin tunnel but, like me, knew little about it. Leary himself had no plans for such a book and so, with his encouragement and help, I began.

In the two years that have followed I have also received indispensable help from many other people. While the documentary backbone of the book is furnished by recently declassified Central Intelligence Agency and National Security Agency documents, the all-important flesh was added through personal interviews with key participants in both the Vienna and Berlin operations. Hayden Peake, an invaluable friend in opening doors in the United States, very quickly put me in touch with David Murphy, whose co-authored book *Battleground Berlin* is an essential starting-point for any study of Cold War intelligence.[1] Unreservedly generous with his help, he ensured that others who could add to the story agreed to talk to me. In addition, he kindly lent me several photographs of the operation, some of which are reproduced here. My debt to David Murphy will be

ix

apparent throughout, although he bears no responsibility for any of my views or mistakes. My thanks, too, go to Walter O'Brien and Hugh Montgomery, both of whom took time to see me and whom it was a pleasure to meet. One other CIA participant in the operation also deserves warm mention. During a regrettably brief visit on my part Joseph Evans gave very generously of his recollections as a member of the tunnel intelligence-processing team in London. This was a significant but hitherto largely unknown dimension of the operation and I am particularly grateful for his help.

If my visit to the United States delivered rich rewards, so did that to Berlin. Here Dr Helmut Trotnow, Director of the Allied Museum, which now occupies part of the former American forces' compound in the city, was unreservedly hospitable, showed me around the museum and led me on an unforgettable walk along the reconstructed section of the spy tunnel now on display. Here I also met Willie Durie, an indefatigable researcher and incomparable mine of information on the history of the allied presence in Berlin. His constant enthusiasm for this project, and the help he has given me particularly, but by no means exclusively, in providing photographs of the tunnel and other Cold War sites in the city, has been one of the genuine and lasting pleasures of the project.

In addition to all the above, I wish also to thank the following friends and colleagues for the help they offered in many different ways: Matthew and Richard Aldrich, Rupert Allason, William Baldwin, Gill Bennett, David Boardman, Tom Bower, Martin Clark, John Crossland, Philip Davies, Tatiana Ershova, Ralph Erskine, Anthony Glees, Michael Gow, Madeleine Haag, Jonathan Hacker, Michael Herman, Christopher Holtom, Alan Judd, David Kahn, Brian Lattell, Timothy Naftali, Ken Robertson, Allen Simpson, David Simpson, Michael Smith, Bob Steers, Donald Steury, Bayard Stockton, Richard Valcourt and Donald Watt.

I would not have been able to write the book without travel and research assistance, and for this I am greatly indebted to both

Acknowledgements

the Faculty of Arts and the Development Trust of the University of Edinburgh, which provided me with grants to visit Berlin and the United States. Both the Institute for Advanced Studies in the Humanities and The Centre for Second World War Studies, in the persons of Paul Addison and Jeremy Crang, provided institutional homes for the book. Grant McIntyre of John Murray offered encouragement throughout, as did my hard-working friend and agent, Andrew Lownie. Matthew Taylor did an excellent job copy-editing the manuscript. My wife, Jeanne Cannizzo, was an enthusiastic backer of the project from the beginning and was an enormous help in every way during my research trip to the United States.

Finally, to all those on the British side of this Anglo-American success who wish to remain anonymous, but who will know how invaluable their help has been in providing the missing Secret Intelligence Service dimension to the story, I express my warmest thanks.

David Stafford
Centre for Second World War Studies
Department of History
University of Edinburgh

June 2001

Introduction

As a schoolboy growing up in the 1950s my first vivid memory of the Cold War was a headline announcing the death of Josef Stalin. It felt as though a shadow had been lifted from my world. Yet all too quickly I became aware of another. The world's first thermonuclear explosion, only a few months earlier, had vapourized an atoll in the Pacific. The mushroom cloud was 25 miles high and 100 miles wide. Then the Soviets exploded their first hydrogen bomb in Siberia and the British detonated one at Woomera, in Australia. The nuclear arms race had begun. Millions were gripped by the fear that they might see the end of the world in their lifetime. Britain, I learned, would have only four minutes' warning of a surprise attack.

Our local newspaper published a map showing the ever-widening circles of damage likely to be inflicted by a nuclear bomb on Newcastle, my home town, from instant vapourization at the centre through a fire zone of incineration to fatal irradiation in my suburb. I pored over it at night in my bedroom. How far and how quickly, I wondered, could my father drive us to safety in our gallant Morris Minor? Assuming we survived the initial blast, what would our death by irradiation be like? Adults resolutely avoided dealing with such questions, perhaps wisely. But weekly shelter drills in the United States were routine. 'Bring a woolly hat', suggested one hopeful leaflet. The American

Director of Civil Defence offered no such comforting illusions. Thirty-six million Americans would die on the first day, he estimated, and for survivors life was going to be 'stark, elemental, brutal, filthy, and miserable'.[1] My vivid adolescent imagination grimly filled in the blanks.

Such apocalyptic visions of nuclear war and surprise attack were also mesmerizing governments and setting the agenda for their intelligence agencies. Tracking the enemy's nuclear and conventional armouries and scanning the horizons for the slightest hint of danger consumed the energies and budgets of spymasters and their agents, both East and West. They competed to devise operations of greater and greater daring that would yield intelligence to provide the vital safety net. Of these, Operation Stopwatch/Gold, the Berlin spy tunnel, was one of the most remarkable.

A bold and imaginative *coup* that made headlines around the world, Stopwatch/Gold was a joint operation between the United States' Central Intelligence Agency and Britain's Secret Intelligence Service. It involved digging a clandestine tunnel, about half a mile long, across the sector border from West to East Berlin to tap into some of the Soviet Union's most closely guarded secrets. Allen Dulles, then head of the CIA, described it as 'one of the most valuable and daring projects ever undertaken'. An engineering triumph, it was preceded and inspired by similar but by now mostly forgotten operations in Vienna.

It was also highly controversial. The KGB had known about the project from its beginning, when its details were passed on by a traitor to his masters in Moscow. The British intelligence officer George Blake was later sentenced to forty-two years' imprisonment for betraying a raft of secrets to the Soviet Union. When he was unmasked in 1961 it was widely assumed that the spy tunnel had been transformed into a vehicle for Soviet deception and misinformation, a complex and ingenious weapon turned against its creators. But the end of the Cold War and subsequent revelations about KGB operations have startlingly challenged this view. It now appears that Stopwatch/Gold did, after all, merit the praise from Allen Dulles.

This is the first full-length study of the Berlin tunnel, which has made appearances as an episode or footnote in general histories of intelligence agencies or of the Cold War, and occasionally in brief articles, but never as a story in its own right. Nor has any other Cold War spy tunnel received detailed attention. Even as I was interviewing my CIA informants about their exploits in the 1950s, news broke of an American spy tunnel built two decades later under the Soviet embassy in Washington DC. Allegedly run by the FBI and the National Security Agency, its mission was to monitor conversations within the Soviet and later Russian diplomatic compound. Robert Hanssen, the FBI officer arrested on espionage charges early in 2001, is believed to have revealed its existence to Moscow. Unwittingly, it is rumoured, the FBI had proudly escorted top brass visitors through the tunnel to show off its electronic wizardry. Once they knew about it, one Washington 'intelligence source' was quoted as saying, the Soviets obviously used it to feed disinformation back to the FBI and the entire operation had been nothing but a gigantic and expensive white elephant and embarrassment to the United States. As for the Russians, they predictably declared that if the reports were true then the operation represented a blatant violation of international law. Yet in Moscow there was a distinct lack of surprise and even a weary sense of déjà vu. 'It is well known', declared Tatyana Samolis, a spokeswoman for the SVR (the KGB's foreign intelligence successor), 'that U.S. intelligence services harbour a passion for tunnelling.'[2] 'Even the hardest of Cold War veterans', reported *The Times* of London, 'may have shivered at the thrill of it all.'

The Berlin tunnel occupies a historic and honoured place in the story of the Cold War. It was a joint British–American operation, in which the CIA and SIS worked closely together. Unfortunately, in each country a national perspective has tended to prevail, obscuring a central element of Stopwatch/Gold.

While the CIA has been relatively open about its Cold War Berlin exploits, SIS, true to British tradition, has remained firmly tight-lipped. The result, inevitably, has been that the tunnel is widely seen as a purely American operation. One aim of this book is to redress the balance and highlight the essential role of SIS in the tunnel's conception, planning and operation. The 'special relationship' between London and Washington is at its most enduring and powerful in the realm of intelligence and, as a masterly recent study has shown, the Cold War intelligence war waged by the West was largely an Anglo-American team effort.[3] Another reason for writing about the tunnel is to address what is likely to become an increasingly common and puzzled question: what was the Cold War all about? The story of Stopwatch/Gold and its Vienna counterparts may, I hope, help answer the question.

NOTE

The Soviet secret service was known by many acronyms throughout its life. For simplicity's sake, I refer to it by its most familiar designation, the KGB.

I

'The Stuff of Which Thriller Films Are Made'

IT IS APRIL 1956, eleven years since Hitler committed suicide in his underground bunker in the garden of his Chancellery. Berlin remains a city of rubble and refugees. The once proud capital of Bismarck's Germany, the metropolis dreamed of by Hitler as the capital of his thousand-year Reich, has had its heart ripped out by allied bombing. Buildings are still scarred from the heavy artillery assaults and bitter last-ditch fighting between Nazi troops and Red Army forces. Acres of bomb sites and mountains of brick and stone disfigure the city centre: at the end of the war Berlin contained one seventh of all the rubble in Germany, some 70 million cubic metres of it.

The Brandenburg Gate, the symbolic heart of the city, stands in a no man's land at the end of the once magnificent tree-lined Unter den Linden, now little more than a desolate street of improvised offices and disconsolate shops. The Reichstag is still a burned-out shell. Hitler's Chancellery, just a few hundred metres away, has long been dismantled to make way for the Soviet War Memorial dedicated to the Red Army soldiers killed in the battle for the city. Every day carefully laid explosives bring another roofless and precarious ruin to the ground.

Physically devastated, the city is also politically stricken, its future unclear. It lies some hundred miles behind the 'iron curtain' that now divides the democracies of the West from the

Soviet satellites of the East. Later in the year boiling discontent in Hungary is to culminate in a popular uprising that brings Soviet tanks into the streets of Budapest and sends tens and thousands of Hungarians fleeing to the West.

Bonn, a small town on the Rhine, has for seven years been the capital of the rapidly recovering western Federal Republic, and Berlin is now claimed as the seat of the Soviet puppet regime, the German Democratic Republic. However, the city is still officially occupied by the armed forces of the victorious powers of 1945: Britain, the United States, France and the Soviet Union. Each controls a separate sector but the Cold War has effectively divided Berlin into two distinct halves, East and West.

The Berlin Wall is still five years in the future. Berliners living in one part of the city still cross over to work in the other, and still visit friends and family there. Yet they do so only at special checkpoints and after showing identity documents. Telephone links have been severed. Only a generating plant provided by the Americans keeps the Western half of the city fuelled with electricity after the East German regime cuts off supplies. The city lives in a half-light of fear, apprehension and suspense.

In camps, in temporary housing flung up around the city or crammed together in overcrowded tenements, thousands of refugees flood into West Berlin from behind the Iron Curtain. Many come from East Berlin and other devastated cities such as Leipzig, Dresden and Chemnitz, now renamed Karl-Marx-Stadt. In 1953 anger against Walter Ulbricht and his regime had exploded in a popular revolt that was crushed by Soviet tanks. Hundreds of demonstrators were killed and thousands more arrested, and East German gaols are still full of political prisoners. Since then the daily count of those fleeing to West Berlin has inexorably risen, but among them are dozens, perhaps hundreds, of spies.

'Go search for people who are hurt by fate or nature', advised the Soviet General Pavel Sudoplatov, commander of the KGB's Special Bureau (Spetsburo) no. 1, when discussing the recruitment of agents.[1] The human debris thrown up by the war has produced regiments of recruits for both East and West. This city, capital of the Cold War, is their natural home. Here they can easily move across sector boundaries in search of information to be traded to the highest bidder. Ian Fleming, already famous for his fictional creation James Bond, explores Berlin for his newspaper, the *Sunday Times*. His informant is an amused and ironical figure who shows him around the city's spy haunts. Fleming identifies him merely as 'O', for he is a notorious middleman selling his information to the highest bidder among the competing Western intelligence services. The living is obviously good, notes Fleming. Herr O is plump and well fed, lives in a 'Hansel and Gretel' villa in the suburbs and chain-smokes expensive Muratti filter-tip cigarettes.[2]

Trade is brisk. Intelligence agencies abound: the United States Central Intelligence Agency (CIA), the British Secret Intelligence Service (SIS), the Soviet KGB, the East German Stasi, the French SDECE and many others. The KGB alone, based at the former St Antonius Hospital in the eastern suburb of Karlshorst, has a staff of almost a thousand. The British SIS is housed in offices attached to the showcase Olympic Stadium constructed by Hitler for the 1936 Olympics. The complex now forms the headquarters of British military administration in the city and a useful, if fairly transparent, cover for the SIS staff of about a hundred. The CIA has recently moved. For years it occupied the former headquarters of Field Marshal Wilhelm Keitel, head of Hitler's General High Command, a quaintly traditional building designed by Hitler's architect Albert Speer in the leafy suburb of Dahlem. But expansion has forced a move to the sprawling United States' military compound on the Clayallee, the broad long highway that forms the backbone of the American sector.[3]

To the south, in a semi-deserted and almost rural part of the sector known as Rudow, the East–West frontier is marked by white-painted wooden posts stuck in the ground. A shanty town of shacks and hovels constructed from rubble and inhabited by refugees has grown up close by. Now and again a patrol of East

German border guards makes a cursory appearance. Running just behind the boundary is the highway linking East Berlin city centre to Schönefeld Airport and flights to Moscow, Warsaw, Prague and other capitals of the Eastern bloc.

Between the highway and the barbed wire on the Eastern side lie an open field and a cemetery. Beyond is Alt-Glienicke, a village within the city still paved with cobbled streets. To the west, about 800 metres into the American sector, stand three low modern buildings in the middle of a field, encircled by two rings of barbed wire. Word on the street is that it is a disguised radar station monitoring Soviet flights in and out of Schönefeld or the nearby military airfield of Johannisthal. Building began two years ago and was quickly completed. American service trucks and jeeps constantly roar in and out. Uniformed soldiers wearing the insignia of the United States' Signals Corps have been spotted on the site. East German border guards sometimes stare at it through binoculars, but the novelty has long worn off. It is just another part of the city's growing stock of Cold War furniture. Nearby, the sails of the city's only functioning windmill turn slowly in the wind.

It has been a wet spring. For weeks heavy rain has been falling on the city, pouring through unrepaired roofs, seeping into cellars and basements still crammed with refugees and the homeless, short-circuiting underground cables and sending repair crews shuttling around the city. Nothing seems out of the ordinary, then, when, at one o'clock in the morning of Sunday 22 April, a team of men arrives at a point on the Schönefelder Chaussee just opposite the radar station and furiously begins to dig at two or three points along the surface.

But the diggers are no ordinary workmen. They come from a special unit of the Red Army, a signals detachment, and they are digging with a purpose. An hour into the dig, and just a few metres below the road surface, they suddenly break through into what appears to be an underground room or chamber. They peer curiously but cautiously down into the dark.

Most of Berlin is still asleep. One of the slumberers is Markus

Markus Wolf, head of the HVA, East Germany's foreign intelligence service, and later to become one of the twentieth century's most ruthless and brilliant spymasters

Wolf, head of the HVA, East Germany's foreign intelligence service, later to become one of the twentieth century's most ruthless and brilliant spymasters. To Western intelligence services he is known as 'the man without a face', for his ability to avoid the camera. Only twenty-nine when he took over the service four years ago, he is thought by some to be far too young and reckless. But he comes from good communist stock, has lived in Moscow, is fluent in Russian and is trusted by the Soviets. In reality his fledgling service is little more than a satellite of the KGB.

Towards dawn he is wakened by his housekeeper. She tells him that the Minister for State Security, Ernst Wollweber, is waiting for him at the garden gate. Wolf has survived enough communist purges to be immediately suspicious of unexpected visitors at night. He grabs the loaded pistol on his bedside table and peers through the curtains. Outside is the minister and an ageing Volkswagen. Mystified, Wolf opens the front door. An emergency summons from the Russians, explains Wollweber: he's had no time to summon his official driver, so has borrowed a neighbour's car. They rattle off towards Alt-Glienicke. There, in the grey dawn light, they see the digging party on the Schönefelder Chaussee. Standing watching them are men whom Wolf instantly recognizes as the top brass of Soviet military intelligence in Berlin.

Using pickaxes to hack through concrete, the soldiers have penetrated the underground chamber. Wolf joins the others in clambering down. The room is the size of a large study, with two chairs and a table in the middle. Bundles of cables, each carefully divided from the others, run along the wall. Each bundle has an amplifier attached to it. Here signals are being picked up, magnified and diverted along cables that disappear down through a trapdoor in the floor. Not until after midday, and endless phone calls to higher authority, do technicians finally remove the door and reveal a shaft leading to a steel-lined tunnel that disappears in the direction of the American radar station.

But Wolf has already seen enough to know he is in the presence of a brilliant intelligence *coup*. The cables being tapped carry some of the Red Army's most secret and most sensitive communications. Among them are messages between Moscow and Wünsdorf, south of the city, the headquarters of all Soviet forces in Germany. It is, he admits with the grudging admiration of a professional, an intelligence man's dream and a technical marvel.[4]

The American press, quick to seize on the drama of it all, thinks likewise. The Soviets are eager to make propaganda out of the affair and within forty-eight hours hold a press conference at the tunnel for the hungry Western media, an unprecedented display of openness in this secretive city. The tunnel, declares a Red Army spokesman, is a blatant act of imperialist aggression and international gangsterism. He points the finger directly at Washington. Journalists and cameramen clamber eagerly down the shaft for a guided tour led by Colonel Ivan Kotsiuba, the Soviet military commandant of the city. He takes them along the tunnel as far as a makeshift barrier made of piled-up sandbags. On top is a notice scrawled crudely in Russian and German:

'You are now entering the American sector.' Flashlights pop, and the picture appears in newspapers around the world.

The joke goes down well with the American journalists. No one is admitting anything in Washington – not at the Pentagon, nor at the State Department, nor at the CIA. But it is easy to put two and two together. Far from being shocked or horrified, the press is delighted. American prestige in Germany has suffered since the failure to help the East Germans during their revolt in 1953. The KGB has carried out a succession of kidnaps. The most dramatic was two years earlier, on the tenth anniversary of the famous bomb plot against Hitler, when Otto John, head of West Germany's new security service and a former anti-Hitler resister, disappeared from West Berlin and resurfaced in the East, denouncing the West and seeking political asylum. Espionage is a game the Soviets seem to be winning. The CIA, after all, is only eight years old. By contrast the KGB traces its lineage directly back to Lenin's Cheka, formed immediately after the Bolshevik Revolution in 1917. Soviet spies have been turning up far too frequently in Washington.

With relief and exuberance the American newspapers bring news of the tunnel to the American people. 'Yankee resourcefulness and ingenuity is not a myth after all', declares the *Washington Post* in unabashed glee under the headline 'The Tunnel of Love'. 'Frankly', writes a leader writer for the *Boston Post*, 'we didn't know that American intelligence agents were that smart.' A *Time* magazine feature article describes it, simply, as the 'Wonderful Tunnel'. But it is left to the *New York Herald Tribune* to sum it all up. Alongside a detailed description of the tunnel and all its technical gadgetry, it declares proudly that the tunnel represents a venture of extraordinary audacity, 'the stuff of which thriller films are made'.

There is no more avid reader of all this coverage than the Director of the CIA himself, the dumpy, bespectacled, pipe-smoking veteran of the intelligence game Allen Dulles. Berlin is close to his heart. Here, as a junior diplomat in the State Department, he enjoyed his first posting, to the Weimar

Republic after the First World War. As a high-ranking official in the Office of Strategic Services (OSS), he spent the Second World War in Switzerland running agents in and out of the Third Reich. When American forces finally reached Berlin in July 1945, it was Dulles who immediately flew in and established its Berlin operations base in Dahlem, subsequently inherited by the CIA. He has been Director for three years. Officially he and the agency are saying nothing. But behind the scenes he relishes the credit.

The publicity is excellent for the agency. Many critics in Congress and the country regard it with suspicion, dubious about the value of its covert operations. Or their morality. Or their expense (for its budgets are secret). When Dulles next visits Berlin, he goes out to Rudow followed by a posse of pressmen. 'What about the tunnel?' they ask. 'Tunnel? What tunnel? I don't see any tunnel', he replies, poker-faced.[5]

Some of the equipment uncovered by the Soviets is clearly marked British. But in London the headlines are focused on something far more newsworthy. The new leaders of the Soviet Union, President Nikolai Bulganin, and the jovial First Secretary of the Communist Party, Nikita Khrushchev, the successors to Josef Stalin, are on an official state visit to Britain. It is the first trip by Soviet leaders to London since the Bolshevik Revolution. Hopes are high that it will mark the beginning of a serious thaw in the frigid political climate. The climax of the celebrations comes on 22 April, with a visit to Windsor Castle and a reception by Her Majesty the Queen.

But the discovery of the tunnel is less than twenty-four hours old and the press conference in Berlin is still to be held. Word comes down rapidly from the Kremlin to the KGB in Berlin that no mention is to be made of any British involvement. Sir Anthony Eden, the Prime Minister, issues a similar instruction to SIS. Nothing should disturb the game of high stakes diplomacy being played out in Whitehall. British diplomats reporting on reactions to the tunnel in Germany and Eastern Europe are kept securely in the dark about their own country's role. So are the British public. The London press remains oddly incurious and discreet. Soon after, the East Germans close up their end of the tunnel and the American buildings in Rudow are eventually abandoned. Before long the tunnel is forgotten.

Yet it deserves to be remembered. As the *New York Herald Tribune* claimed, its story possesses all the excitement of a first-rate thriller. And like all good Cold War thrillers, the story begins in another place and at another time. For this, in reality, is a tale of two cities.

2

Our Man in Vienna

IN 1948 A new SIS head of station arrived in the Austrian capital, Vienna. His name was Peter Lunn and he was destined to become a central character in the story of the Berlin Tunnel. A trim, soft-spoken man, slightly built and with piercing blue eyes, he was still in his mid-thirties. Later, after years of observing him at work, the KGB would describe him as a cautious and experienced operative who placed a high priority on security with his agent contacts. Lunn was described by his Soviet counterparts as 'demanding'; he 'strives to give his agents set tasks and to ensure they are carried out clearly. He is very economical when paying rewards . . .'[1] He also brought a wealth of experience and contacts to his new position.

Lunn had already made a name for himself as a championship skier. 'Talkative, argumentative, sociable, a man who slipped down a slalom with ease', was how one fellow skier fondly remembered him. Lunn first put on skis at the age of two and the mountains were his natural terrain; as a boy of eight he poised proudly to be photographed standing next to the famous mountaineer Andrew Irvine.

In 1936, the year of the Berlin summer Olympics, Lunn was named captain of the British ski team. The winter games that year offered the first real chance for the Third Reich to show off its athletic and organizational prowess to the world at large. Held

Peter Lunn, the charming and sociable SIS chief in Vienna and Berlin who masterminded the tunnel operations seen here in Bonn in 1957

Peter Lunn's risk-taking and competitive edge were honed as captain of the British Olympic ski team – seen here in Mürren, Switzerland, in 1936. Lunn is third from the left

at Germany's principal alpine resort, Garmisch-Partenkirchen in Bavaria, events took place in a purpose-built stadium for 150,000 spectators positioned dramatically beneath the Zugspitze, Germany's highest mountain peak. In a driving blizzard regiments of singing Hitler Youth, Nazi labour battalions and sports organizations marched through the streets. In the stadium Hitler, hatless in the snow, received a tumultuous welcome as he presided over the opening ceremonies and march past of national teams.[2]

Ostentatiously, Lunn absented himself from the proceedings. 'I got a lot of credit for this, which was totally undeserved', he recalled later, 'I happen not to like marching about.' Skiing remained his passion. In the year that he took over the SIS station in Vienna he also coached the British team for the 1948 winter Olympics in St Moritz. To toughen himself up he even put on his ski boots and clumped around the narrow maze of streets outside SIS headquarters in London, situated in an office block on Broadway across from St James's Park underground station, in the heart of Westminster.

Skiing was a family affair. His grandfather Sir Henry Lunn had single-handedly developed the sport of winter skiing, turning the Swiss resort of Mürren into a British enclave and founding the travel agency that bore his name. (Mürren, ironically, was later to provide the location for the filming of *On Her Majesty's Secret Service*, the most forgettable of the James Bond films.) Sir Henry's son Sir Arnold Lunn, Peter's father, continued the tradition and in addition became a high-profile convert to Roman Catholicism and Christian controversialist in the 1930s. Lunn himself, the elder of Sir Arnold's two sons, joined the family firm a few years after leaving Eton, learned German, and then spent much of the Second World War in Malta.

Ostensibly he was working for the British Council. But it is difficult to imagine what this cultural agency, best known for organizing speaking tours of visiting authors and artists, was doing on this besieged Mediterranean island, and his position was almost certainly a cover for SIS. Indeed, Lunn's own *Who's*

Who entry claims he entered the SIS in 1941. In 1945 he was
posted to Italy, where he passed a parachute course. 'I shall always
remember parachuting as the activity which provides maximum
fright with minimal risk', he recalled. After the war he worked
in Germany running the all-important Hamburg station. He
returned to London in 1946 and as 'P [Production]3' he supervised the SIS stations in Austria and Germany, now on the front
line of the rapidly developing Cold War battle with Moscow.

Lunn was a complex man, for whom physical exertion and
danger possessed an almost spiritual dimension. The author of
several handbooks on skiing, he once listed the pleasures of the
sport as precise technical execution, the thrill of speed, and self-
mastery. In the triumph of mind over body, argued Lunn, the
skier could catch a fleeting glimpse of 'that paradise that was our
ancestors' in the Garden of Eden'. Yet fighting Nazism and wit-
nessing its results in Germany taught him that such worship of
the body and its physical prowess could too easily be perverted.

At the end of the war Lunn wrote a novel of love, passion,
blackmail and murder, entitled *Evil in High Places*. Set in the
Swiss Alps on the eve of war, it features a villain who climbs
mountains to escape from his feelings of inferiority, at first literally and then symbolically as he comes eventually to look down
on his fellow men and to decide who should live and who should
die. The analogy with Hitler gazing down at the world from his
Eagle's Nest above Berchtesgaden is clear. But Lunn's novel also
echoed G.K.Chesterton's short story *The Hammer of God*, about
a man who says his prayers from the top of a church tower and
then begins to look down on the world rather than up to God.
A devout and committed Catholic, like his father, Lunn readily
embraced SIS's post-war mission of fighting the Soviet Union
and communism. In Vienna his energy and commitment to
technical skill found a new and intriguing outlet.[3]

★

If there was a serious competitor to Berlin in the post-war spy
stakes it was Vienna. Since the end of the First World War the

city had suffered turbulent times. Stripped of its status as grand imperial metropolis by the collapse of the Habsburg empire, by the 1930s its streets provided a bloody battleground for bitter fighting between left and right. Then, in 1938, it witnessed the wildly cheering crowds that embraced Adolf Hitler as he arrived to annex the land of his birth.

Seven catastrophic years later Vienna fell to the Red Army and was placed under four-power occupation. The historic centre of the city inside the Ringstrasse, the great inner boulevard that encircles the main government buildings, was placed under joint four-power control. Once a month each of the occupying powers took charge of security and sent out patrols consisting of four military policemen from each power: an incongruous and volatile mix ripe for linguistic misunderstanding. Beyond this inner core the city's remaining districts were apportioned into American, Soviet, French and British zones, marked only by notice-boards and separately policed by each of the powers. The Soviet districts soon became dangerous no-go areas of arbitrary arrests and kidnappings. To add to the perils, zones were not always contiguous, so that moving from one British district to another could involve crossing Soviet-controlled territory. This mosaic created bizarre absurdities, such as the order to all British personnel to proceed immediately to British headquarters in the city at the first sign of Soviet attack – a route that would have taken many of them right through the Soviet sector.

Like Berlin, the city was peopled by spies and wrapped in intrigue. When Red Army commissars held sole control of the city in 1945 they took the opportunity to pack the police with communists. Soviet agents had been slipped into political parties and the postal and telegraphic offices had been deeply pene- trated. 'A sinister feeling of menace hung over the city', recorded Suzanne Fesq, an Englishwoman working for the Allied Control Mission, 'stalking the streets and pervading the air so that you didn't even feel secure in your own home. At any time of the day or night a great battering on the door could bring doom and disaster. People, once kidnapped, were never heard of again . . .

and the very few who did escape, never dared tell.' Richard Helms, a future CIA Director and at this time director of plans in Washington, once briefed an agent on his Vienna mission. 'The KGB is looking right down our throats', he said, 'and they're playing for keeps – you can bet your hat and breakfast that they will double or kidnap any agent they spot.'[4]

By the time Lunn arrived in Vienna the climate had only marginally improved. Many of the communist police had been fired but others remained in place, especially in the Soviet-controlled districts, where they formed a dangerous fifth column in the restored Austrian republic. Nationwide elections in 1945 had decisively rejected the communists. This merely fuelled their efforts to gain power by subversive means. Early in 1948 Czechoslovakia fell to the communists after a sustained campaign of internal attack. This was no faraway country but a next-door neighbour whose fate was all too visible. Events in Prague sent a chill through Austria. Weeks later the opening skirmishes of the Berlin blockade cast a further ominous shadow. Vienna, like the German capital, lay deep within the Soviet-occupied zone. Its citizens braced themselves for a communist *coup*.[5]

The landscape was ideal terrain for high-tension Cold War drama. Lunn's Vienna was captured for ever on screen by *The Third Man,* the classic film based on the novel by Graham Greene and starring Orson Welles. The author himself had spent the war working for SIS in Sierra Leone and London. Early in 1948 he flew to Vienna to seek background detail for his tale of Harry Lime and the sordid black market trade in diluted penicillin.

The smashed and dreary city presented a miserable sight. Days of artillery bombardment and heavy street fighting between desperate SS divisions and the forces of Marshal Tolbukhin's Third Ukrainian Front had taken their toll. Rubble lay everywhere, and pedestrians had to weave their way carefully along the still littered streets. Steel rods hung like stalactites, rusty girders formed skeletons in the snow, and the Kärntnerstrasse, the once elegant main shopping street, consisted of a single-storey row of patched and battered shops. Black market restaurants were serving up little more than soup and bones. Many Viennese were collapsing on the streets from hunger. There was virtually no entertainment; most theatres had been destroyed by bombing. The Stefansdom was a virtual ruin, pockmarked from shelling.

In the Russian-controlled part of the city the Prater, the vast amusement park along the Danube whose huge Ferris wheel provides a centrepiece of *The Third Man*, was a scene of desolation. Weeds grew in profusion, the foundations of merry-go-rounds resembled huge abandoned millstones, rusting tanks lay where they had been abandoned, and there were shell-holes everywhere. Only the great wheel itself was intact, standing against the skyline as one of the city's few great landmarks left untouched.[6]

Below ground existed an equally sinister and dangerous world. Searching for a plot, Greene discovered through SIS contacts the existence of an underground police whose job was to patrol the vast system of sewers. The entrances above ground were disguised as advertisement kiosks and remained unlocked. Below there were no zones of occupation, and agents could slip undetected from one part of the city to another. This provided Greene with the famous scene in which Harry Lime first gives the slip to his pursuers above ground and then finally, in the dark below, meets his end. The sewers, noted Greene, smelt curiously sweet, like ozone. Their policemen, it turned out, wore lint-white uniforms, like ski instructors.[7]

Lunn would undoubtedly have been intrigued by the comparison. Once established in Vienna, he also turned his gaze from the snow-peaked mountains to life below ground. But he was less interested in the sewers than in another target: the underground cables that carried telegram and telephone traffic in and out of the city.

★

The Berlin blockade put both British and American intelligence on full alert for any signs of a Soviet attack on Western Europe. Austria stood on the European front line, and Vienna was a vital forward listening post. Red Army troops occupied the eastern half of the country as well as the capital. To the north and east, Czechoslovakia and Hungary were both now firmly in Moscow's grip. Tito's communist Yugoslavia, already straining at Stalin's tight leash, lay to the south. If and when Soviet tanks rolled, Austria would be a principal battlefield.

In Vienna, Soviet headquarters operated out of the grand old Imperial Hotel on the Ringstrasse. Here, with the hammer and sickle flag flying from its rooftop, the KGB and GRU (Soviet Military Intelligence) occupied the top floor. The city, in the words of one KGB man, was 'an operational playground for Soviet intelligence whose officers were never deterred by the Austrian Government from obtaining visas or meeting recruited and potential agents'. CIA officers called the Imperial 'the honey pot'.[8] For telegraph and telephone communications with their central group of forces in Austria, as well as with Moscow and the outside world, the Red Army and KGB relied on cable networks built in the nineteenth-century heyday of the old Habsburg empire. Squarely in the European tradition of state monopolies, the entire system was run by the Austrian Post Office.

As the KGB noted, Lunn was particularly effective at running agents: demanding, giving them set tasks, ensuring these were carried out clearly and paying out rewards only if he had to and if he was certain the intelligence could be used. Vienna in the late 1940s provided a surfeit of agents and a feast of information. Pouring into Lunn's office in the British embassy, where he officially held the title of Second Secretary, came a stream of reports about Soviet troop movements and military installations. But nearly all of them were based on visual information and added up to an essentially superficial picture. What Lunn needed was a high-placed source inside Red Army headquarters or the Soviet high commission.[9]

One day he was sitting in his office leafing through a pile of reports provided by one of his agents with contacts in the central post office. Sudddenly Lunn's eye was caught by a particularly intriguing piece of information. Several of the cables linking the Red Army to Soviet units and airfields in eastern Austria ran through the British and French sectors of the city. Lunn realized that if they could be tapped and their conversations recorded he could uncover the intelligence so urgently demanded by London and Washington about Soviet mobilization and the possible start of World War Three.

Such material would be useful not just to SIS but also to the many other agencies eagerly shopping around for information. High on the list was army intelligence, with its myriad of officers and units scattered throughout the British zone. Its Field Security sections needed to identify Soviet spies and agents threatening their work. Field Security has been described as 'the sharp end' of military intelligence and its motto, veterans wryly claim, should have been 'first in, last out'. During the Second World War Field Security agents were frequently the first to enter a captured city to secure vital buildings and arrest their opposite numbers, and when the army moved on they tidied up the loose ends of intelligence affairs.

The fighting was over but the Cold War was keeping them busy and their role had expanded. Now, as part of the occupation forces, they were working with other services, such as SIS. In Vienna, housed on two floors of a nineteenth-century apartment block on the Sebastiansplatz, they targeted industrial and military developments behind the Iron Curtain.[10] They also had their hands full interrogating illegal frontier crossers, or IFCs. Plenty of the desperate were still finding their way across the ploughed fields and barbed wire entanglements along the borders with Hungary and Czechoslovakia. After weeding out the fake refugees and communist plants, Field Security milked them for military and industrial intelligence about Eastern Europe. Phone tapping was an integral part of its repertoire. Even as Lunn was dreaming up his Vienna operation, allied counter-intelligence in Trieste was running – hidden behind a door discreetly labelled 'Cabinet Office Historical Section' – an extensive telephone tapping operation into Yugoslavia.[11]

The Americans were also busy. Field Security's American equivalent was the US Army's Counter-Intelligence Corps, or CIC, and its units in Austria, such as the 430th Detachment, played fast and loose with similar Cold War missions. 'There were no guidelines,' recalled one of its veterans, 'we and the Russians just made up the rules as we went along.'[12]

Lunn's army of agents had little difficulty in getting hold of blueprints of the city's cable network. Most of the cables ran underground and so tunnels became the obvious route of attack. Lunn now began to assemble the team of experts he needed for the operation. It was to involve several separate digging operations or tunnels in the city, each of which would provide inside information about the Red Army in Austria. If Stalin gave the order to invade Western Europe, Lunn would be one of the first to know.

His immediate boss at SIS headquarters in London was Andrew King. An experienced veteran of European operations, the Cambridge-educated and wealthy son of an officer in the Argyll and Sutherland Highlanders had been one of the earliest recruits to the so-called 'Z' network of pre-war British intelligence agents. This was the inventive creation of the controversial SIS mandarin Claude Dansey, otherwise known as 'Colonel Z'. From its base on the eighth floor of Bush House in London, the 'Z' network provided a parallel to the 'mainstream' SIS networks in case they were penetrated or rolled up by the Germans. Many of its agents operated under the commercial cover of such firms as Unilever and Royal Dutch Shell.

King knew Vienna well. Soon after Hitler's Anschluss the Nazis had uncovered Dansey's existing agent there, the central European correspondent of the *Manchester Guardian* Frederick Voight. King was sent out to replace him. His cover was provided by Alexander Korda, the film producer, who was also Dansey's closest collaborator and whose company, London Film Productions, received secret service money. But the ruthless grip of the Gestapo ensured that Vienna was largely hostile terrain, and after the outbreak of the war King moved to Zurich and Geneva, and eventually Berne.[13]

Now King was in charge of all operations in Austria, Switzerland and Germany, and was to be intimately involved with both the Vienna and Berlin tunnels. When Lunn eventually left Vienna, King replaced him as head of station. He made a colourful impression on those who met him. One of them was the then novice MI6 officer Anthony Cavendish, who in 1989 successfully defeated a government effort to suppress his highly controversial memoirs *Inside Intelligence*. In 1951 Cavendish was stationed in Vienna, ostensibly as a member of the Austrian Control Commission but in reality as liaison officer between military intelligence and the SIS contingent in the embassy. In his memoirs he talks unfavourably of King, whom he disguises as 'Philip', a man, he writes, 'who gave the impression of being homosexual'. King was a man of peccadilloes, claimed Cavendish, not the least of which was taking 'an unhouse-trained little Pekinese' around with him. Another colleague still vividly remembers that in the drab and still impoverished Vienna of the early 1950s King cut a remarkable figure by ostentatiously riding around in a large, chauffeur-driven Jaguar car.[14]

But for Lunn, mobilizing Andrew King and SIS headquarters was not enough. He knew that he needed to clear his plan with the Foreign Office as well. As luck would have it, the former chairman of the Joint Intelligence Committee, the London apex of the system, had recently been transferred to Vienna as British high commissioner. This was the robust and forthright Harold Caccia, later to become a highly effective and popular British ambassador in Washington. A keen shot and good sportsman, Caccia had taken the measure of the Foreign Office and guessed it would veto such a daring *coup*. So he decided not to tell them. Instead, he gave Lunn the go-ahead on his own initiative. 'I couldn't look at myself if there'd been an invasion and I denied the chance of getting the information', he confessed later.[15]

The largest and most renowned of Lunn's Vienna tunnel efforts was undoubtedly the one dug in the suburb of Schwechat. It lay in one of the British sectors to the south of the

*Andrew King, SIS chief in Vienna during Operation Classification and
London SIS point man for the Berlin tunnel, was always noted for his love of
fast cars. Here he is seen at the wheel with a friend in Munich in the 1930s*

city and just beyond the terminal of one of the main tram lines.
Here ran one of the underground cables linking the Imperial
Hotel with the nearby city airport and Soviet military headquar-
ters for Austria in St Pölten.

But how to dig a tunnel and install a tap without anyone
finding out? Lunn took a look around the neighbourhood and
decided the safest way would be to purchase a house close by.
From there, out of public view, SIS could burrow away.

A large and comfortable villa with an extensive garden and big
trees, the house had a lengthy driveway leading down to the

main road. The neighbours undoubtedly noticed when a young married couple who obviously worked for the British military government moved in some time later that year. They were sociable and lively, and threw lots of parties that often went on until the early hours of the morning. Nor would their Austrian neighbours have missed the gang of workmen who arrived soon afterwards to resurface the driveway. What they could not have guessed was that the cheery young major who had taken possession of the villa was the right-hand man to Peter Lunn for his daring scheme. Nor that the driveway resurfacing was vital preparation for the digging of a tunnel from the villa out to the cable that ran along the roadway outside.

The major's name was John Edward Wyke. Those who knew him remember him as a dapper ballroom dancer with an eye for the ladies who in later life turned his hand to writing radio plays for the BBC. But the reality of his life was even richer in drama. Wyke was a veteran of the wartime Special Operations Executive (SOE), created by Winston Churchill in 1940 to 'set Europe ablaze' by carrying out sabotage and subversion behind enemy lines. Wyke, commissioned as a captain in The Queen's Regiment, spent most of the war in the Middle East working on SOE operations in the Balkans, if his official file is to be believed. At least one person who later knew him claimed that in early 1945 Wyke, who was part Dutch, had also been involved in dangerous SIS intelligence operations conducted from the liberated part of the Netherlands into the northern, German-occupied zone.[16]

But special operations were still needed after the war and SIS took over the job, along with many of SOE's staff, including Wyke. During the transition period, early in 1946, SOE's thousands of files were either kept, weeded or simply tossed out. Wyke was one of those in its Central Archives Section who decided their fate. He approached the task with a dashing verve that bordered on recklessness. In the half-deserted old Baker Street headquarters of SOE, sitting with his chair tipped at an angle and his feet on the desk, he would pore over the mountains of files. Behind him was a large waste-paper basket. He would pick up a file, nonchalantly glance at the title, rapidly reach a decision and then, with the flick of a practised wrist, consign the condemned documents over his shoulder to bureaucratic oblivion.[17]

But within the devil-may-care Major Wyke was a cool professional. Since joining SIS he had become the in-house expert on the delicate art of phone tapping. At the end of the 1950s he was to distinguish himself by braving terrorists in Cyprus to climb a telephone pole in pitch darkness and place a tap on the telephone line of Archbishop Makarios in an effort to trace the EOKA guerrilla leader George Grivas.[18] Later, in the 1960s, he successfully installed an intercept on the telephone lines of the ill-fated King Idris of Libya. But for now, smartly turned out in his uniform and with a swagger stick under his arm, his efforts were focused firmly beneath Vienna.

To help him, and to round out the tunnel team, Lunn brought in two other experts from London. One was a private mining consultant of considerable experience known as Colonel Balmain. He agreed to take charge of building the tunnel and construct the tap chamber, where the delicate final stage of connecting up with the cables would take place. The other expert was John Taylor, a small sharp-faced man with a pencil moustache who had served as a communications officer with Montgomery's Eighth Army in North Africa. Taylor ran technical research operations for SIS and MI5 from a cramped laboratory inside the top secret Special Investigations Unit of the Post Office. This workshop of tricks and devices was located in an ugly redbrick Victorian building at Dollis Hill in north London. Taylor's task was to bring in Post Office personnel to assist with all the detailed technical aspects of the operation. His own personal energy was largely concentrated on what turned out to be one of the most difficult problems of all: the penetration of moisture into the multitude of circuits being tapped.[19]

With Wyke, Balmain and Taylor on board, Lunn was ready.

The overall code name given to the Vienna tunnel operations was 'Classification'. The one out at Schwechat was also christened – in honour of Wyke's expansive lifestyle – 'Lord'. None of those involved suspected at this stage that Vienna was only the start of something very much larger, which would eventually take them all to Berlin.

3

Smoky Joe's

IT LOOKED LIKE any of the other rows of boarded-up old shops that littered post-war Vienna. Perhaps their owners had died, or been transported, or had simply given up in despair in the impoverished city. The three single-storey buildings stood for-lornly on the Aspangstrasse, a short cobbled street practically opposite the main railway freight station in a British district of the city. No one gave them a second glance.

Yet for deserted shops they had a curious number of visitors. These would arrive singly and glance cautiously around before entering the front door of the middle shop. At the rear of the shop the visitors pressed a bell beside another door made of bul-letproof steel. This door had a spyhole and behind it wooden stairs descended steeply to a cellar, with three uniformed soldiers on duty with Sten guns. One of them climbed the stairs, peered through the spyhole and, when he was satisfied by what he saw, swung the door inward so it opened across his body. Down below, the other two had strict orders to fire in case of any doubt: the visitor might be being followed. At the bottom of the stairs was a small room lined with packing cases which disguised yet another door, which also opened inwards. Behind it lay a different world.

Crammed into the concealed space sweated half a dozen men. During the day only a paltry light filtered in through six thick glass bricks. At night the cellar's denizens worked with a couple of bare light bulbs. Beyond them in the gloom stretched a short tunnel, no more than three or four metres long, which ran out from the basement under the road outside. Dug by a unit of the British Army's Royal Engineers, it lay just a metre and a half below the cobblestones. A jungle of wires hanging down from a portion of exposed cable lying under the road led to three telephone switchboards. A row of tape recorders lined an inner wall. Men with earphones listened in carefully. The cable being tapped carried telephone lines. Whenever the eavesdroppers heard a conversation begin, they isolated the relevant line and turned on a machine which recorded the talk on old-fashioned Edison wax cylinders. Six inches long and two inches in diameter, every now and again these had to be shaved with a device like a pencil-sharpener to expose a fresh surface. Alongside was a calibrated strip of paper.

As soon as a call came through, one of the men started a recorder and noted the telephone line, and the time, on the paper strip. Most of the conversations were in Russian. Many of the speakers had the curious habit of first blowing down the mouthpiece of the telephone, as if issuing orders from the bridge of an old ship to the engine room below. The lines being tapped carried all local Soviet military telephone calls, as well as long-distance civilian traffic to cities behind the Iron Curtain such as Budapest, Bucharest and Sofia. These, too, were occasionally used by the Red Army. Each morning the used wax cylinders were picked up in a laundry basket and taken for processing to the headquarters of Int. Org., or British Military Intelligence, which formed part of the British military headquarters complex based at the Schönbrunn Barracks in the city. From here items of special interest were sent on to Government Communication Headquarters (GCHQ) in Britain.

The operation had begun in the autumn of 1948, when British intelligence was contacted by a telecommunications expert in the Austrian government. Did they know, he asked, that a cable under the Aspangstrasse carried Soviet military traffic? Even more valuable was his information about a 'blister' on the cable, a point where cables had been soldered together, which made phone tapping easier. The British occupying forces requisitioned the shop premises shortly afterwards for ostensible use as an RTO, or railway transport office, a plausible enough cover given the close proximity of the freight marshalling yards. After digging the tunnel and removing the soil to the garden of a large house occupied by Field Security across the city, the sappers were promptly posted to the other side of the world, Singapore.

Listening in was boring and repetitive work. It carried on, round the clock, with three men at a time working two- or three-hour shifts and the off-duty men sleeping on makeshift beds next to the telephone switchboards. Most came from the British Army's Field Security section.

The work was anything but glamorous. There were long, dreary periods when none of the lines was in use. Boredom in the cramped dark basement stretched everyone's nerves. To fill in the time and to lessen the tension, the soldiers talked office gossip, sex, sport, food.

One of them was Bob Steers. A regular in the Intelligence Corps, he had spent the previous two years interrogating refugees and running small-scale intelligence operations along the Italian and Yugoslav frontiers. It had been exciting work and he was ill equipped for the tedium that confronted him in Vienna. 'So', Lunn greeted him, 'now you're in Vienna you think it's going to be all wine, women and song. Well, let me tell you, old boy, it's all beer, bitches and broadcasting.' It also meant hours of boring eavesdropping, although there were some surprising compensations under the Aspangstrasse. 'Every night', he recalled,

we used to listen to what we called 'The 2 o'clock Jump'. In those days the band led by Stan Kenton had a popular jazz record entitled 'The One o'Clock Jump'. At this time the traffic was very light and the telephonists in the various capitals (Vienna, Budapest, Bucharest, Sofia) would chat to each other. These conversations would be put over a speaker in our cellar so that everyone could enjoy them. Intimate sex lives would be discussed, especially by the ladies on the Vienna and Budapest exchanges, and it certainly broadened our youthful perspectives of life.

In between times these callow young eavesdroppers munched chocolate and smoked the endless supply of cigarettes provided free by the army. In the unventilated and claustrophobic space the air was always thick with smoke. Mixed with the smell of bodies and the oozing basement damp, it made for an acrid and noxious climate. But this was the Cold War, and they were stationed on the front line. They called it Smoky Joe's.

This was the first of the Vienna tunnels. To arrange and supervise the tap SIS sent the telephone tapping expert John Taylor and two assistants out from London. Their arrival almost caused the operation to come to grief before it began. They travelled by train wearing military uniform and disguised as members of the British occupying forces. With them, in packing cases, they carried all the sophisticated technical equipment they needed for the task. It had been arranged that the railway transport officer at the Aspangstrasse would meet them and escort them to the site. 'For some reason he did not', recalled Steers, 'and the travellers phoned the Sebastiansplatz to say they had alighted in Wien-Meidling, which was in the Russian sector.' The station was crawling with Soviet military police, the last place a team about to install a top secret tap on Red Army communications should be. Quick-footed work by Field Security extricated the Post Office team, which they found standing forlornly on the platform in unfamiliar battledress and surrounded by packing cases containing their top secret technical equipment. Beside them Russian military policemen patrolled the platform. It was a tricky situation and could have blown the operation from the beginning.

Field Security was all too aware of the security aspects. 'The operation was TOPSEC', recalled Steers.

Politically speaking it was arguably one of the most sensitive plans ever carried out by the Int. Corps . . . one tiny slip could have resulted in massive international reverberations. All discussion on the tapping was forbidden outside the cellar and even the other personnel on the City Detachment were ignorant of the work of their confreres. All details of one's civilian friends had to be submitted for vetting.

Even when it was up and running Smoky Joe's came close to disaster. The Aspangstrasse was a main thoroughfare for heavy goods vehicles bound for the freight station. The gradual pounding of the trucks caused the roadway above the tunnel to sag. Some sharp-eyed Austrian Post Office maintenance worker noticed this. One quiet Sunday morning, when the traffic was light, a three-man investigation team arrived unannounced on the scene. Bob Steers can still remember the high state of alarm below ground as the workers sniffed around on the street above.

Looking out, I saw to my horror three Austrian workmen with pickaxes attacking the area in the road above our tunnel. We had a 'panic' telephone on which one did not speak. I lifted it up and replaced it on the bridge. This alerted the security officer on duty at Sebastiansplatz and he automatically knew what action to take. Within the hour, and with the workmen getting closer to our tunnel, the GOC [General Officer Commanding] Austria arrived with the Austrian equivalent of the Postmaster General. I know what he said because I interpreted for him. 'You see what we are doing here', he said, showing him our setup, 'now, call your men off and if you ever breathe a word about this, I promise you, you will be dead within the hour.'

The repair team vanished as quickly as it had arrived.[1]

A nosy Viennese Miss Marple also came close to sniffing out the secret. In 1952 a young Royal Marines subaltern attached to

SIS in Klagenfurt, in the British zone of Austria, was sent up to Vienna to help out with some digging and roadworks connected with one of Lunn's underground enterprises. He and a young SIS officer assisting him were temporarily boarded out with an eccentric landlady in the south of the city. To explain his mud-caked shoes, the SIS man hastily explained he played football. Each night, as the two men returned home caked in mud, she would ask, with rising incredulity as the week went on: 'Wieder Fussball spielen, Herr Oberleutnant? Wieder Fussball?' ('Playing football again, lieutenant? Football again?').[2]

Smoky Joe's was officially code-named Conflict and ran until 1951, when it was suddenly closed down. The reason was simple. The Soviets stopped using the cable for military traffic and switched to alternative lines. With the drying up of any useful intelligence Smoky Joe's had outlived its usefulness. But was the Soviet decision to discontinue its use fortuitous, or the result of something more disturbing? Had they got wind of its operation? Had someone betrayed it? One of the Vienna tunnels was eventually blown by the British traitor George Blake, but not, apparently, this one.

In addition to Smoky Joe's, British intelligence in Vienna initiated at least two other spy tunnels, which remained at work until Russian and British forces left the city in 1955, when Austria regained its sovereignty. One, code-named Sugar, operated under the cover of a British firm dealing in imitation jewellery and trading under the name of Gablons.[3] The other was the Lord tunnel, which ran from John Wyke's house. According to Anthony Cavendish, then working at the Schönbrunn barracks as liaison officer with Lunn's SIS team in the embassy, this carried on successfully reporting on the Soviet order of battle in Austria until it was abruptly terminated as the result of an accident. 'A tram passing over the tunnel ', recalled Cavendish, 'suddenly caused [it] to collapse and the tram to sink into the resulting deep depression. The whole matter was hushed up but that was the end of the operation.'[4]

If Cavendish's memory is accurate, the incident was probably covered up in much the same way as the episode in the Aspangstrasse. Many of these Cold War operations in Vienna will remain obscure as long as the CIA and SIS keep a lid on them. And for as long as they do so, inaccurate and often apocryphal stories will flourish.

One such tale, much repeated and embellished, surrounds Operation Lord. Casting around for a cover for the operation, so the story runs, SIS first set up a Harris Tweed import shop in a building close to the road, confident that such quintessentially British goods would not attract enough customers in Vienna to interfere with the real business at hand. To its dismay, however, Harris Tweeds proved inexplicably popular among the post-war Viennese, and SIS soon found itself buried beneath an avalanche of import licences as its harassed agents struggled to keep pace with consumer demand. SIS then decided that the first set of tapes recorded by the intercept team should be collected by a British officer from a schoolgirl who would be carrying them in her bookbag while strolling in the city's Schönbrunn Park. Unfortunately, when the British officer approached the young girl, a Viennese policeman arrested him on suspicion of child molesting. Only the intervention of higher authority saved him from further embarrassment.

An amusing story if true, and well worthy of some Graham Greene novel. But it immediately raises some awkward questions. Why, for example, would SIS need the cover of a Harris Tweed shop when they had John Wyke's house to hand? And would they really have trusted such secret and sensitive material as the phone-tapping cylinders to the wayward habits of a schoolgirl? On reflection, it sounds like some bar room tale gleefully told to highlight the curious ways of the eccentric British, and indeed the source of the story turns out to be an American – and one, moreover, who was demonstrably unreliable.

★

The Americans were as deeply involved as the British in the game of espionage and counter-espionage in Vienna. They, too, focused wary eyes on the 100,000 men of the Red Army's Central Group of Forces poised for possible attack against the West from their own zone of Austria. For the CIA, Red Army headquarters at Baden bei Wien offered an obvious target. Eventually, in 1952, they recruited a significant mole there in the shape of Lieutenant-Colonel Pyotr Popov, who gave them valuable material on the Soviet order of battle.

But until then Austria and Vienna were barren territory. 'At the time', writes the former CIA operative William Hood in his study of the Popov defection, 'firsthand information on the USSR was so hard to come by that the lowest, dog-faced private deserting from the Red Army was considered a valuable source and immediately flown out of Austria to a defector centre in Germany.' Pressure on the CIA to deliver early warning of Soviet attack was as intense as that on SIS in Britain. The day a new CIA deputy head of station was being sent out to Vienna he was summoned into the Washington office of Richard Helms. 'Our basic job is to penetrate the Soviet establishment', declared Helms, 'that's the only way to get the answers the White House is screaming for. One penetration agent will be worth a ton of the scraps we're getting from those so-called spies – the guys on the outside looking in.'[5]

But there were other ways of penetrating the Soviet establishment, and cable tapping could provide vital data on Soviet intentions. Information about the role of the Americans in the Vienna tunnel operation, so far as it has publicly surfaced, rests almost exclusively on the account of a man named Carl Nelson, who worked for the CIA's Office of Communications, the section specializing in phone tapping and other technical tricks.

In the 1970s Nelson was interviewed by the Washington-based journalist David Martin for his book *The Wilderness of Mirrors*, about the self-destructive suspicions and personal rivalries about Soviet penetration that almost destroyed the CIA. Here Nelson claimed to have arrived in Vienna in 1951 to explore how Soviet landlines could be tapped. Lunn and SIS had kept the CIA completely in the dark about their operations, and

Nelson independently began to investigate the location of Soviet landlines. He started outside the Red Army's headquarters in the Imperial Hotel, noting a couple of cables linking it to the Soviet command in Moscow. 'He strolled through the streets', wrote Martin, 'following the path of the cables overhead to the outskirts of the city, where they snaked underground to connect with the long-distance lines leading to Moscow.' On a map he had acquired of the city's cable system Nelson then traced their underground route as they ran parallel to the main highway connecting the Vienna airport to the city centre. This task accomplished, he then searched for a suitable site to make a phone tap. But before he had succeeded SIS found out. They took him aside and informed him of their own operation at Schwechat. At that point, according to Martin's account, the CIA joined forces with Lunn's team in a joint Anglo-American operation which the Americans code-named Silver.[6]

Yet Nelson's account has been vigorously contested by other CIA operatives. Some claim that he was not even in Vienna at the time. Others describe him as 'brilliant but erratic', a man they would not trust to tell any story straight. And indeed, the stories themselves appear highly implausible. But Nelson went on in his interview with Martin to make two further bold and extraordinary claims.

The first is that it was his discovery of the cables in Vienna that forced SIS to share their hard-earned intelligence with the Americans. This is highly misleading. Intelligence gleaned from Vienna was already being passed on to the Americans at higher levels. What did happen was that at some point after Lunn's operations began, and after he had left for another posting, the CIA was brought into the scene. The details of how exactly this happened still remain obscure, hidden away in files not yet open. But the general outline can now be revealed.

Under Lunn the local CIA station in Vienna had been kept strictly out of the picture. As a result it had begun its own independent operations to identify Soviet cables, as claimed by Nelson, although Nelson himself was not part of them. Then, somewhere, there was a high-level leak, probably accidental, to the CIA, and SIS had little choice but to bring in the Americans. Soon after, Lunn's successor Andrew King arrived 'in a sweat' at the Vienna CIA station headquarters to let them into the secret. By some extraordinary coincidence the American he had come to brief, a man named Bronson Tweedy, turned out to have been at the same British preparatory school as King. This schoolboy friendship eased what might otherwise have been a frosty reception. As a result, King took the CIA station's two most senior officers out in the back of a British army truck to look at one of the SIS tunnels in action. From then on, recalled one CIA veteran, 'we were on board'.

The broad gist of Nelson's claim that SIS initiated the Vienna tunnel operations and that the CIA joined them later is correct. But another far more startling claim is not. According to Nelson, while the Russians were carefully enciphering their cable messages, an echo of the original, non-enciphered plaintext could be picked up using special equipment – provided the intercept was made no more than twenty miles or so from its point of origin. Nelson described this as the 'echo effect' and claimed to have discovered it while testing the security of an American cipher machine known as the SIGTOT, manufactured by Bell. 'No codebreaking was required', reported Martin, based on his conversation with Nelson. 'Once he had hooked up the proper combination of capacitors, amplifiers, and assorted gadgets, Nelson could sit back and watch the clear text clatter forth at sixty words per minute onto an ordinary teletype machine.'[7] The discovery immediately forced a prompt modification of the SIGTOT system and adoption by the Americans of a far more secure machine.

Nelson claimed that, studying the Vienna traffic, he realized that plaintext echoes (or 'transients') of the messages being transmitted to and from the Imperial Hotel could be sorted out from the encoded signals being monitored in the tunnel at Schwechat. Such a discovery made code-breaking largely redundant and was obviously a major breakthrough. 'American intelligence', claims

Martin, 'had scored its biggest coup since the wartime codebreak that had uncovered source HOMER' (the British KGB mole Donald Maclean). But Nelson also claimed that the British were not let in on the echo effect. Many authors have repeated the claim, such as John Ranelagh in his major history of the CIA *The Agency*, which relies heavily on Martin's account of Silver.[8]

If true, Nelson's claim suggests a breathtaking lack of trust between allies. On the surface it may seem plausible, fitting in as it does with a drama being played out simultaneously on the broader intelligence stage. The year 1951 saw the infamous defection to Moscow of Maclean and another high-ranking British diplomat, Guy Burgess. Coming shortly after the cases of the British scientists Alan Nunn May and Klaus Fuchs – both convicted of betraying atomic secrets to Moscow – the defections sparked a high-level molehunt. Suspicion quickly fell on Kim Philby, the SIS liaison man with the CIA in Washington. Although nothing could be proved, Philby was recalled from the United States and shunted off into some harmless dead end to spend most of the next decade under cover as a stringer working for *The Observer* in Beirut. Only in 1963 did SIS finally have firm evidence of his guilt and send one of its senior officers, Nicholas Elliott, to confront him. The head of station in the Lebanese capital by this time was none other than Peter Lunn, and it was to Lunn's private flat that Elliott invited Philby to come and 'chat'. Within days, realizing the game was finally over, Philby had fled to Moscow.

Curiously, the suspicion that fell on Philby in the aftermath of the Maclean and Burgess affair also clouded the career of Andrew King, who was summoned back from Vienna to London to be questioned in depth by Dick Thistlethwaite, one of MI5's most practised interrogators. What worried MI5 was the discovery that King had been a member of the Communist Party while an undergraduate at Magdalene College, Cambridge, the university where Burgess and Maclean had been recruited. King readily admitted the charge. But he also told Thistlethwaite that he had previously revealed all this to Kenneth

Cohen, the SIS controller of European operations, some four years before. Cohen, after consulting the head of the service, Sir Stewart Menzies, had told King not to worry about it'. '"C" says', Cohen allegedly said, 'that since spies are only people of foreign origin, don't bother.' This put King in the clear, and he returned to Vienna to continue work on the tunnels.[9]

Did news of King's interrogation leak out to the CIA? And, if so, did this persuade them to hold back on Nelson's discovery about the so-called echo effect in Vienna and not share it with their allies? Certainly, the Burgess and Maclean defections, followed by the Philby affair, persuaded many inside both the FBI and the CIA that the British services were riddled with Moscow's men. Was the Vienna tunnel yet another victim of the Cold War paranoia that turned allies into dangerous suspects?

It seems unlikely. For one thing, Nelson's claim about the echo effect surfaced only once, in his conversation with David Martin. No other author has made any such grandiloquent claim about American triumphs against Soviet signals during this early phase of the Cold War. Indeed, it is possible that Nelson deliberately told his tale to conceal the extent of more traditional code-breaking successes against the Russians. Those who knew him suggest that he was prone to exaggeration anyway, but also speculate that genuine confusion and misunderstanding may have arisen.

There is no doubt that the echo effect could be found in certain situations. But where it did, British intelligence, with its far longer experience of line tapping than the Americans, certainly knew about it. And Nelson noticeably failed to provide any information on how, in practice, American technicians working cheek by jowl with British colleagues could have concealed the fact that they were capturing the plaintext message from the same set of cable messages being tapped by their allies.

CIA colleagues of Nelson have also strongly contested his claim. One of them, provoked by Nelson's bizarre claim, directly broached the issue with Frank Rowlett, the Chief of Staff D and Nelson's boss. Rowlett insisted there was no such effect in the telegraphic traffic being picked up in the tunnel operations. The only adjustment made to the signal in processing was, in Rowlett's words, 'a straightforward conversion of the recorded signal on the tape to a format which could be interpreted by a teleprinter'. The device that performed this demodulation for the CIA was called the 'bumble-bee' and had been designed by one of Nelson's subordinates, using commercially available parts. All aspects of the telegraphic material, stressed Rowlett, were discussed fully and openly with SIS. The 'echo effect' as a factor in CIA–SIS relations over the Vienna and Berlin tunnels is an enduring but insupportable myth.[10]

★

Lunn's phone-tapping operation in Vienna soon began to produce enormous volumes of Russian conversation on tape. To cope with translating material from the mounting pile of wax cylinders SIS provided two fluent Russian-speakers from London. But they were quickly overwhelmed. The problem was not just the volume but the often highly technical nature of the material they had to handle. The answer lay in finding native speakers of Russian, and a large number of them, quickly. Yet to station such a team in Vienna would attract unwelcome attention and pose an unacceptable security risk. So SIS decided to relocate this side of the operation to London.

The Broadway headquarters already housed a small unit, known as 'N', which squeezed out intelligence from the conversations of foreign diplomats whose phones were being tapped by MI5. But the section's tiny space could not be enlarged and was staffed by elderly linguists who were unable to cope with the heavy and constant flow of material from Vienna. SIS therefore created a new and more important section, known as 'Y'. The Lunn operation was growing faster and larger than anyone had ever imagined.

4

Black Friday

WHILE THE EAVESDROPPERS pursued their clandestine tasks beneath the streets of Vienna, Cold War shadows rapidly darkened the landscape above. Stalin's blockade of Berlin sparked a major war scare. Fears of a surprise Red Army attack in Europe gripped Washington, where bitter and traumatic memories of Pearl Harbor remained fresh.

The CIA had just been created. Hurriedly cobbled together from the remnants of such wartime agencies as 'Wild Bill' Donovan's Office of Strategic Services (OSS), it had not yet moved into its now famous headquarters at Langley, Virginia. That was to happen only a decade later, during the great Cold War crises over the Berlin Wall and Cuba. Instead, its burgeoning army of Cold War pioneers found themselves housed in offices scattered around in downtown Washington, many of them prefabricated huts hurriedly thrown up after Pearl Harbor along the reflecting pool in front of the Lincoln Memorial.

Despite its later focus on covert operations, the agency's main function was to provide early warning of enemy action. 'I don't care what it does', declared George C. Marshall, the Secretary of State, 'all I want from them is twenty-four hours notice of a Soviet attack.' The CIA came out of the 1948 Berlin blockade with its reputation enhanced. Unlike General Lucius D. Clay, the commander of American forces in Germany, who was convinced the blockade heralded an imminent Soviet invasion, it asserted correctly that the Red Army was not ready to march.[1]

The end of the blockade did little to assuage fears. Throughout Eastern Europe, helped by the KGB and accompanied by purges, show trials and the mass imprisonment of dissenters, Stalin's puppets tightened their grip. The creation of two rival German states turned Berlin, the one remaining gap in the Iron Curtain, into an El Dorado for the intelligence services of all sides. In 1949 the Soviets successfully detonated an atomic bomb, while China fell to Mao Tse-tung's communists. The next year Korea exploded into a hot war and set off a spiralling arms race.

In Washington, London and Moscow intelligence chiefs were briefed urgently to make warning of a surprise attack their top priority. 'Preventing the worst was the most important job for us', recalled Markus Wolf, head of East Germany's foreign intelligence army during most of the Cold War. He described his task many years later as being 'to prevent surprises, above all military surprises. That was the main job.' To motivate his forces he even personally wrote the German lyrics of one of the Stasi's inspirational songs – a Russian import – 'The Soldiers of the Invisible Front'. [2]

Germany was the main battleground of this new war. Here British intelligence officers also felt the heat. At this time the largest SIS base in Europe was at Bad Salzuflen, a spa town in the British-occupied zone of Germany roughly half-way between Osnabrück and Hanover. Anthony Cavendish began his intelligence career there. 'We lived with an ever-present threat that the Red Army could overrun us within forty-eight hours if the rumours of war became a reality', he recalled. The Bad Salzuflen base controlled networks of agents throughout the garrison towns of East Germany, with orders to report any signs of a Soviet build-up. Watchers on the East German railway system recorded the numbers of flatbed railcars they spotted, which might be used for transporting tanks. Agents on the Polish and Russian borders noted the movements of Soviet military vehicles, wrote down the numbers painted on the sides of tanks, and transmitted the information back to SIS on bulky Second World War vintage wireless sets.[3]

All was grist to the mill of analysts in London struggling to sketch a picture of Soviet military capabilities in Eastern Europe. But they were floundering. This was made graphically clear to a young navy scientist attached to the Marconi Company, named Peter Wright. One dismal spring day in 1949, as the rain drummed down on the tin roof of his prefabricated laboratory in Essex, he was summoned to an urgent meeting in Whitehall. Waiting for him, along with scientists from the laboratories of other services, was Freddie Brundrett, the chief scientist at the Ministry of Defence.

'Gentlemen,' declared Brundrett when they were all seated, 'it is quite clear that we are now in the midst of war.' Events in Berlin had made a profound impact on defence thinking. But the war they faced, stressed Brundrett, would not be fought by soldiers – at least not in the short term – but by spies. Yet here the situation was far from promising. It had become virtually impossible to run agents successfully behind the Iron Curtain and there was a serious lack of intelligence about Soviet intentions. To fill the gap, technical and scientific initiatives were urgently needed.

Thus was Peter Wright – later to become infamous for his best-selling memoir *Spycatcher* – recruited into MI5 as its first research scientist. His top priority was to develop 'new techniques of eavesdropping that did not require entry to premises'. As he left the meeting, another government scientist came up and introduced himself. It was John Taylor, the telephone-tapping expert from Dollis Hill, who was already deeply involved in the Vienna tunnel operations. 'We'll be working together on this', he said, 'I'll be in touch next week.'[4]

★

The same Cold War pressure led to President Harry Truman's decision early in 1950 to order a wide-ranging review by the National Security Council (NSC) of American strategy and the world scene. The result was an apocalyptic report numbered

NSC–68, which declared that America was 'mortally challenged' by a Soviet Union that was animated by a fanatical faith which would impose itself on the world unless deterred by a massive build-up of American arms. In addition, the enemy should be weakened from within by an intensfied campaign of covert economic, political and pyschological warfare.

This was a key document in the Cold War. Adopted by Truman, it provided the guiding light for American policy towards Moscow for the next decade. Soon afterwards, Field Marshal Sir William Slim, the renowned wartime commander of Britain's Fourteenth (and 'forgotten') Army in Burma, and now Chief of the Imperial General Staff, returned in a sombre mood from a visit to Washington. The United States, he confessed to colleagues, was 'convinced that war was inevitable [within] the next eighteen months'.[5]

NSC-68 also called for 'the improvement and intensification of intelligence activities' to provide warning of Soviet attack. This understatement barely masked a quiet desperation in Washington. Just five years before, American and British codebreakers had been cracking top-grade enemy ciphers and providing prime intelligence about Germany and Japan. Now they were failing abysmally to crack Soviet ciphers.

There was only one noteworthy success. The Venona project broke ciphers used by the KGB with its agents inside the United States and elsewhere during the war. The almost 3,000 messages intercepted by Venona were to reveal startling details about Soviet espionage and led to the unmasking of several communist agents. The most notorious of these were the atomic spy Julius Rosenberg and his wife, Ethel, who were sent to the electric chair in 1953 amid a chorus of worldwide condemnation.[6]

Venona has been described as 'the greatest secret of the Cold War'. Yet it was a retrospective project, begun in 1944, which threw light on past rather than current Soviet activities – although it provided a vital touchstone for Western counter-intelligence in evaluating the accuracy of current intelligence acquired from Soviet defectors and other sources. 'Unlike Ultra,' confessed Sir Dick White, who uniquely headed both MI5 and SIS during the Cold War, 'where we knew the inside of the German High Command, we never got inside the Russians through Venona.'[7]

But so far as Cold War traffic was concerned, advances were small. Ciphers used by the Soviet armed forces, police and industry yielded some results, and by 1948 American and British code-breakers were between them reading six Red Army ciphers and a number of diplomatic and naval and police ciphers.[8] Much of this story remains secret even today. But documents released in September 2000 by the National Security Agency – since 1952 the principal American code-breaking service – claim that this effort was building 'a remarkably complete picture of the Soviet national security posture'.[9] If so, it still fell drastically short of what was needed. High-grade Soviet ciphers remained unbreakable. In addition, American code-breakers were plagued by frustrating inter-service rivalries between each of the armed services' separate code-breaking agencies, a lack of resources and a serious sapping of morale.[10]

Then, in October 1948, catastrophe happened. A Soviet mole was working at the very heart of America's code-breaking campaign in the army's security agency at Arlington Hall, Virginia, a former girls' high school just across the Potomoc. His name was William Weisband. The son of Russian immigrants, he had joined the army code-breakers during the Second World War as a Russian linguist. But he had been working secretly for the KGB, where he enjoyed the code name Zhora ('Link'). The friendly and gregarious Weisband made it his business to roam around the agency's offices learning everything he could of its work. 'He cultivated people who had access to sensitive information', said one of his colleagues. 'He used to sit near the boss's secretary who typed everything we did of any importance.'[11]

Weisband met his KGB handler at a restaurant just outside Washington. On meeting days he smuggled documents out of Arlington Hall under his shirt, first during his lunch break and again at the end of the day, and hid them in the boot of his car.

After a while he asked for a camera so that he did not have to carry documents. The KGB refused on the grounds that this made it more likely he would be caught. Soon after, Weisband did indeed fall under suspicion and the KGB paid him off with $1,694.00 and a permanent password for use if they ever contacted him again. They never did. Nor did Weisband confess to his treachery when confronted by the FBI. He dropped dead of a heart attack a few years later, still under suspicion.

One of the first secrets Weisband betrayed was Venona. Then he revealed allied successes against other Soviet codes. KGB files in Moscow acknowledge that from Weisband the Soviets learned that 'important data concerning the stationing of the USSR's armed forces, the productive capacity of various branches of industry, and work in the field of atomic energy' was now compromised.[12] Kim Philby, Moscow's high-placed mole in Britain's SIS, who was briefed on Venona, did likewise. The result was that on 29 October, a Friday, the Russians executed a massive shift of their cryptographic systems. Newly released NSA documents reveal that all high-level Soviet radio networks, including mainline military nets, were changed to the unbreakable one-time pad system. All Soviet ciphers being read by the Americans and British were taken off-air. They also changed their standard radio-operating procedures to make Western interception far more difficult.

Then, over the next few months, Moscow carried out another major change that blinded the West even further. They shifted as many of their signals as they could from wireless to landlines, both above and below ground, which were considered far more secure. Dismayed, allied code-breakers on both sides of the Atlantic lumped these disasters together under the designation 'Black Friday'. In the words of a National Security Agency history, it was 'perhaps the most significant intelligence loss in U. S. History'.[13] The same could be said for Britain. NSA and GCHQ worked in tandem. Throughout this period an American Venona expert, Joan Callahan, was working alongside British colleagues at Government Communications Headquarters, the peacetime successor to Bletchley Park. Meredith Gardner, the guiding genius of the Venona project, succeeded her.

Because of Black Friday American code-breakers failed to provide any advance warning of North Korea's attack on the south in 1950. From then on President Truman lived in dread that he would receive no advance warning of a Soviet attack elsewhere. Germany, especially Berlin, seemed the most likely target.

The CIA could do little to help. As Freddie Brundrett had revealed to the meeting in Whitehall, the growing impenetrability of the Iron Curtain made the missions of human agents increasingly perilous. While Washington tried to prompt resistance inside Stalin's European empire, these cloak-and-dagger operations threw little light on the prospects of a Soviet attack. Tightening vigilance by the communist secret police severely limited what high-placed sources could deliver. There was a terrible sense of frustration throughout the burgeoning intelligence community in the American capital. 'Intelligence is inconclusive as to whether or not the Soviet intention is to precipitate a global war now', confessed the CIA dispiritedly.

Frustrated and fearful, Truman demanded a vastly improved code-breaking effort to deliver high-grade intelligence. One of his final acts as president was to approve the creation of the National Security Agency. The day he signed the document that brought it into being the Democrats lost the 1952 presidential election to the Republican candidate, Dwight D. Eisenhower. Before long the NSA's budget and personnel were far outstripping those of the CIA.[14]

5

The Human Factor

'BLACK FRIDAY' DID more than just hasten the creation of the National Security Agency. By blinding allied code-breakers and leading to a Soviet shift from wireless to landlines, it forced the West to cast around for alternative ways to decipher Moscow's intentions. Instead of aerial messages yielding rich intelligence harvests, perhaps more terrestrial efforts should be tried. For all the importance of signals intelligence (Sigint), traditional agent operations such as those being run by the CIA still had a vital role to play. Inadvertently, William Weisband had set in motion forces that led to one of the most audacious operations of the Cold War.

In Washington one of those who took Black Friday most personally was a thickset, bespectacled and fastidious Virginian in his early forties, Frank Rowlett. 'I can see him standing in a doorway', one of those who worked with him still recalls, 'a pipe clamped between his teeth, scratching his back against the door and speaking with the voice of a good old southern boy.' But his manner, along with his lazy drawl, belied his import. For Rowlett, a trained mathematician, was America's greatest living code-breaker, 'a wizard in making and breaking codes' and the man who had almost single-handedly produced its greatest intelligence prize.

In the 1930s Rowlett had led the team that successfully cracked the mysteries of 'Purple', the Japanese diplomatic cipher machine. As a result, throughout the Second World War the

*American code-breaking genius, the mild-mannered and pipe-smoking
Frank Rowlett, at his desk in Washington, DC, in 1948*

allies had enjoyed a unique and invaluable inside view not just
into Japanese diplomacy but also into top-level Nazi thinking.
Intercepts from Magic – the well-chosen code name for this
miraculous source of intelligence – included detailed reports to
Tokyo by the Japanese ambassador in Berlin, Baron Hiroshi
Oshima, on his discussions with such Nazi leaders as Foreign
Minister Joachim von Ribbentrop and even Hitler himself.
Oshima had also reported in detail on a fact-finding tour he
made of Germany's Atlantic Wall defences in 1943, manna from
heaven for allied planners. George C. Marshall, then chief of staff
to the US Army in Europe, had described Oshima's reports as
'our main basis of information regarding Hitler's intentions in
Europe'. In addition to conjuring up Magic, Rowlett had also
created 'Sigaba', the highly secure American encryption
machine that defied all German and Japanese efforts to crack it.[1]

The Cold War now transformed Rowlett into a leading warrior of the invisible front. His skills were in greater demand than ever, especially after the signing of the UK–USA pact in 1948, a still top secret code-breaking pact with Britain and its leading Commonwealth partners, Canada, Australia and New Zealand. As chief of intelligence for the US Army's Security Agency, he ran Arlington Hall's communications and cryptanalysis operations until the creation of the National Security Agency, and was briefed on Venona from the start. He then served as special assistant to a succession of its directors and eventually became the first commandant of its National Cryptographic School. Honours were showered on him and he received many awards for distinguished national service, including the National Security Award and Legion of Merit, not to mention the OBE from Britain.[2]

By 1951 Rowlett was deeply frustrated by the loss of Soviet wireless traffic. One day he gave vent to this feeling while talking to a friend in the CIA. Perhaps this was where the agency could help, he badgered him. After all, its task was to carry out clandestine missions overseas. If it could locate and tap into Soviet landlines, then Rowlett and his team of code-breakers might be able to read the Kremlin's mind as they had so brilliantly penetrated that of Berlin and Tokyo only a decade before.

It was a bold idea which instantly appealed to Rowlett's friend. His name was William (Bill) King Harvey, and he worked in the agency's Office of Special Operations, the 'command bunker' of America's secret war. Harvey remains a legendary and bizarre figure in the rich and colourful gallery of CIA Cold War heroes. 'Harvey was odd-looking,' remembered the FBI's Robert Lamphere, one of those who worked with him most closely, 'with protruding eyes and a pear-shaped body. His voice was like that of a bullfrog; once you'd heard it – and the intellect behind it – you never forgot it.' An overweight, hard-drinking ex-lawyer from small-town Indiana, Harvey had spent several years in the FBI before leaving under a cloud after crashing his car one night on Washington's Rock Creek Drive following a drunken party. Every day, he liked to boast, he had a different woman.

*Bill Harvey, CIA chief in Berlin who oversaw the tunnel, affectionately
known as 'Harvey's Hole'. Here he is being presented with the Distinguished
Intelligence Medal for Operation Stopwatch/Gold
by his boss, CIA Director Allen Dulles*

It was an image both real and carefully cultivated. Harvey
described himself as a 'three-martini man' at lunch and often fell
asleep at his desk. Colleagues remembered him as the only CIA
officer who always carried a gun. He often left the pearl-handled
revolver conspicuously on his desk, as if he expected to be assas-
sinated, and would frequently load it or work the action in front
of startled visitors. He refused to check it in at restaurants or
embassies. 'Look,' he would say, brandishing it in his sweat-
stained armpit, 'when you need 'em, you need 'em in a hurry.'[3]

But Harvey's outward crudity masked a shrewd and penetrating mind and a highly developed sense of security. A CIA personal evaluation once described him as being 'less than outgoing

on information about operational matters in which he is engaged'. It was a quality that stood him in good stead at the time of the assessment. For by that time – in 1962 – he was heading the ultra-top secret CIA programme code-named ZR/RIFLE, for the planning of 'executive action' (otherwise known as assassination) against targets such as Fidel Castro and the Congo's Patrice Lumumba.[4]

As the FBI's counter-intelligence expert on the Soviet agents identified by Venona, Harvey had been among the first Americans to finger Kim Philby as a Soviet mole. He had come to know Rowlett through the Venona project and he responded eagerly to his friend's latest challenge of another clandestine attack on the Soviets.

Within weeks the CIA had ordered a special study of Soviet landlines in Europe. The task was given to the agency's Office of Special Operations (OSO), the division in charge of running clandestine operations in the field. This in turn gave the mission to its Staff D section, charged with targeting foreign communi-cations overseas. With Harvey providing the driving force inside the agency, behind the scenes Frank Rowlett masterminded the project as head of Staff D. To keep a personal eye on things he moved from his office at the NSA over to the CIA, where he reported to Richard Helms, then the CIA's Chief of Operations and later the agency's head. When Allen Dulles became the agency's new Director in 1953, Rowlett became his 'special assis-tant' and briefed him frequently on the tunnel. In effect, he was overall director of the operation, one of the small handful of people in CIA headquarters who even knew of its existence. Security-conscious to a fault, Rowlett died in 1998 with most of his extraordinary successes still unknown to the outside world.

★

One of the earliest heralds in Europe of Rowlett's master plan was a lean, athletic and tough-talking lawyer and ex-baseball player from Chicago named Walter O'Brien. A law graduate from Wisconsin, O'Brien had spent the Second World War in the infantry before shifting over to military intelligence after American forces crossed the Rhine, interrogating suspected Nazis and becoming fluent in German. Now in the CIA, where his first post had been in Zurich posing as a lawyer, he arrived in Berlin ostensibly as head of the base's counter-espionage division. With his wartime background he seemed a natural choice to his office colleagues in Dahlem.

But they were wrong. O'Brien's position was only a cover for his real mission, which was to scout out the scene for a determined attack on Soviet communications. No decision had yet been made to dig a tunnel, and Harvey was as interested in the possibilities presented by overhead lines as underground cables. He rapidly decided to rely on O'Brien as a trusted and secure officer.

'After we'd done one or two things together', remembered O'Brien, 'Bill suddenly said to me one day that I was "Landsmann". He liked giving people nicknames and with German soldiers *Landsmann* means compatriot, the guy you'd like to ride shotgun with, the fellow you'd trust with your life, your buddy. So I guess I passed the test.' O'Brien knew next to nothing about communications. But what he loved and excelled at was recruiting agents. 'It's a sales job, really', he mused later. 'My father was a sales manager and it wasn't much different. The challenge comes in hooking a guy to work for the American government.'

One of O'Brien's first recruits was an agent who lived in Schwerin, in the Soviet-occupied zone of East Germany. 'He came regularly to see me in Berlin', recalled O'Brien, 'and I was explaining about the overhead lines when he suddenly said there was one right under the window of his apartment. So he had a go and hooked something up to the line. We got loads of material. But they couldn't decipher it, and that was that.'[5]

O'Brien had better luck with agents he recruited inside the West Berlin post office, who were in charge of operating long-distance telephone lines. Most had worked in the once unified German telephone system and kept in touch with former colleagues now working in the East. They could help him identify and recruit agents in the Eastern half of the city who knew how the Soviets were using the system. Not even his boss, the head of the Berlin base, knew of O'Brien's mission. This high-level secrecy even within the CIA was to characterize the operation for the whole of its life.

Berlin was the nexus of Europe's communications systems. On the eve of war in 1939 almost a hundred international lines crossed German territory, and despite the ravages of war all long-distance telegraph and telephone services in Berlin to each of the country's occupation zones resumed in 1946. But ultimate authority lay with the Allied Control Council and the 1948 blockade of the city led here, as elsewhere, to a division. The city's main telegraph office already lay in the Soviet sector. In April 1949 the Soviets also took control of all telephone trunk lines into East Germany – some 93 of them – by opening their own telephone exchange in Berlin-Lichtenberg.

The Lichtenberg exchange offered a prime target for O'Brien. The recruitment of local agents in East Berlin became essential. One of them worked in the long-distance department at Lichtenberg and provided record books that revealed which subscribers were using which underground cables in its area. O'Brien would meet him just across the sector border, drive off with the books to the CIA office in the Western half of the city, have them quickly copied in a photo lab set up in the attic and then return them to his contact before anyone noticed they were missing.

One of his most significant agents was known simply as the *Nummer Mädchen*, or 'Numbers Girl'. She too worked in the East Berlin post office, where her job was the highly classified one of assigning specific long-distance cables for official use and switching users from one cable to another. Detailed records were kept on cards of the current East German or Soviet user of each cable. These cards, carefully numbered, eventually found their temporary way to O'Brien's attic laboratory. Despite strenuous efforts by historians and others to find her, the identity of this Cold War heroine remains unknown. When asked by the author if he remembered her name, O'Brien pointed out that it had been unknown even to him, as she was recruited through a cut-out (or intermediary) to preserve her anonymity.

Yet another of O'Brien recruits was a lawyer in the East German Ministry of Post and Telecommunications, the ministry in charge of the entire East German telephone network, an expert on how the Soviets used the international telephone service in East Germany. Two major Soviet bases heavily depended on it. One was Karlshorst, the KGB headquarters. The other was Zossen-Wünsdorf, a sprawling military complex of offices, barracks, and underground concrete bunkers to the south of the city begun under the Kaiser and transformed into the wartime headquarters of Hitler's Army High Command. In 1936 it had been connected to a complex state-of-the-art underground cable system linking all the military installations that ringed the capital. Although heavily bombed by USAAF and RAF planes during the battle for Berlin, by 1953 it had been sufficiently rebuilt to act as headquarters for the group of Soviet forces in Germany.

Another person willing to help was the same ministry's principal Russian-language interpreter, who was involved in high-level technical dealings with the Soviets. O'Brien also made recruits in telephone offices in East German cities such as Dresden, Erfurt and Magdeburg. To identify potential sources he also relied on interrogating refugees, who were daily flooding into the big detention centre at Marienfelde in West Berlin. Combined with purloined maps showing the exact location of underground cables, all this intelligence eventually gave O'Brien a comprehensive picture of the Soviet communication system in Germany and how it worked. It was clear that it could yield high-grade intelligence. He knew this for certain because yet another of his agents in the East Berlin telephone office agreed to carry out a dangerous experiment.

One night in January 1953, some time between 11 p.m. and 2 a.m., when the office was almost deserted and he could operate without being detected, the agent switched Soviet telephone traffic on to a cable attached to a West Berlin circuit. This gave the CIA a precious fifteen-minute sample of prime target circuit, which was recorded by one of O'Brien's technical experts posing as an employee of the West Berlin post office. They carried out several more similar experiments over the next few weeks. The longest continuous sample was twenty-nine minutes. But most were two- or three-minute snatches. None the less, after analysing the material the Berlin CIA office declared that it was 'unique material of high interest'.[6]

Harvey immediately informed CIA German headquarters in Frankfurt, his principal channel and line of command to Dulles. Staffed with well over a thousand operatives, it was the biggest and most important CIA station outside Washington. Heading it was the 'tintype handsome' and polo-playing General Lucien King Truscott, a battle-hardened Texan who had stormed ashore at Anzio, commanded the American landings in southern France and driven an armoured division across the Rhine into Germany. 'I'm going to go out there and find out what those weirdos are up to', he promised when Allen Dulles's predecessor, Walter Bedell-Smith, sent him to Frankfurt to rein in some of the more gung-ho CIA operations being run out of Germany.

But Truscott was impressed by the tunnel after being briefed by one of his senior officers, nicknamed 'Fleetfoot' by Harvey after his frequent habit of speeding up the autobahn to Berlin.[7] Truscott officially notified Washington that the cables carried Soviet military, KGB and diplomatic telephone and telegraph traffic to and from various Soviet headquarters in Germany. 'In certain instances', he declared, 'it also carried messages between Karlshort and Wünsdorf and Moscow.' It was the spring of 1953. The scene was set for the Americans to repeat and even to surpass Peter Lunn's success in Vienna.

6

2 *Carlton Gardens*

MEANWHILE IN LONDON the changing political scene had put Winston Churchill back into 10 Downing Street. At seventy-seven his powers had waned but he remained formidable, visibly rejuvenated by the adrenalin rush of office. His predecessor, Clement Attlee, an anti-communist hawk, had been just as ready to co-operate with Washington on the Cold War intelligence front. After serving as Churchill's trusted deputy throughout the war he knew almost as many Anglo-American intelligence secrets. It was Attlee and his Foreign Secretary, Ernest Bevin, who had given the green light to the UK–USA code-breaking pact.

But Churchill brought new edge to the quest for intelligence about the Kremlin. He had saved his nation once before. Driving him now was a fierce will to preserve it from nuclear destruction. War, he told the British people during the election campaign, was no longer a romance but would mean nothing less than the massacre of human beings by 'the hideous force of perverted science'.

Almost his first move in office was to set sail on the *Queen Mary* to visit Truman and rekindle the fires of the wartime special relationship. In Washington, for the third time in his life he addressed both houses of Congress. He reminded the packed rows of senators and congressmen of Bismarck's remark that the supreme fact of the nineteenth century was that Britain and the

United States spoke the same language. 'Let us make sure', declared Churchill, 'that the supreme fact of the twentieth century is that they tread the same path.'[1] Early in 1953 the arrival in the White House of his old wartime comrade-in-arms and commander of allied forces at D-Day, Eisenhower, furthered his enthusiasm for marching in step with the Americans. Good intelligence would be essential for the road they trod.

Churchill feared that Stalin might accidentally or even deliberately provoke war in Europe, especially over the still bitterly contested future of Germany and Berlin. To his defence and intelligence chiefs he issued a stream of orders for the earliest possible hint of Soviet attack. 'What is the opinion of the Chiefs of Staff about whether there is any more danger at the present time and how the harvest and weather fit in?' he anxiously inquired over the summer of 1952.[2] His advisers hedged their bets. They assured him that there was nothing to suggest any imminent aggression, and certainly no sign that the danger had increased. On the other hand, they pointed out, total war could still result if the West was forced to respond to some local Soviet action.[3]

Churchill continued to demand data. Reports on Soviet bloc military production, the size of the Soviet budget, the consumption of finished steel in the Soviet Union suitable for armaments and on the new 'Sverdlov'-class cruisers that came into service with the Soviet navy in 1951 landed regularly on his desk. They induced as much anxiety as reassurance. Naval intelligence reported confidently that the Soviet navy was still far inferior to the combined navies of Nato. Yet its future potential should not be underestimated. The Director of Naval Intelligence even stressed that in the face of intense Soviet security measures it was becoming 'progressively more difficult to gather intelligence'.[4] No wonder Churchill was nervous. Even the most comprehensive of estimates made by the Joint Intelligence Committee provided no strategic guidance on the likelihood of general war or on Moscow's willingness to take a gamble on some local offensive.[5]

Churchill was acutely aware that Britain's code-breakers were working in the dark, or at least a crepuscular half-light in which the shape of targets was only dimly perceived. Only a few years earlier, Ultra – the rich intelligence harvest reaped from code-breaking – had kept him informed on a daily basis of Nazi plans through the stream of intercepts that poured in from Bletchley Park. Churchill called this source his 'Golden Eggs'. But now the code-breakers, about to move to Cheltenham under the title Government Communications Headquarters (GCHQ), were no longer laying premium-quality eggs. They worked hand-in-glove with the Americans in efforts to crack Soviet codes and Black Friday had been a disaster for them too.

News of this catastrophe had reached Churchill, even though he was in opposition when it happened, through his former intelligence contact the dashing young former naval attaché in Madrid Alan Hillgarth. During the war Churchill and Hillgarth had worked closely on a cloak-and-dagger operation funnelling millions of dollars through New York to keep Spain neutral. Hillgarth had retired but still stayed in touch. Sometimes he visited Chartwell, Churchill's country home in Kent, where for reasons of secrecy Churchill carefully ensured his name was never recorded in the official guest book.

More often Hillgarth kept him informed in a series of written reports based on leaks from friends still actively involved in intelligence. Information on what was happening inside the Soviet Union was deteriorating, reported Hillgarth on the eve of Churchill's re-election. The code-breakers had failed to crack any significant Soviet ciphers, only some minor codes. The West possessed only a sketchy Soviet order of battle. Such was the dismal picture as the 1950s began.

As soon as he entered Downing Street, Churchill demanded an intensified intelligence offensive to find out more. Many of those who had directed Britain's wartime machinery were still oiling its Cold War wheels. Kenneth Strong, a tough-minded Scot who had cut his intelligence teeth fighting Michael Collins' Sinn Fein guerrillas in the 1920s and risen to become

Eisenhower's personal intelligence adviser during the D-Day landings, was now running Britain's Joint Intelligence Bureau. Sir Edward Travis, head of Bletchley Park at the end of the war and a chief negotiator of the 1948 UK–USA treaty, was still in charge of the code-breakers. But if traditional code-breaking was not working, other ways must be found. Churchill knew this because it had been impressed on him by Hillgarth. Ultra had made British intelligence lazy. A radical reassessment of methods was now needed, urged Hillgarth. However powerful the West was, he told Churchill, 'even a giant is blind in the dark'.[6]

Secret flights over Soviet territory to take high-level reconnaissance photographs were one solution, but they were risky. Attlee had hesitated but Churchill robustly gave them the go-ahead. American Tornado aircraft based at British airfields, but repainted with RAF markings and flown by British and American aircrews, were soon penetrating deep into Soviet territory, equipped with high-powered spy cameras. If one of the planes was detected or shot down, it could cause a crisis with the Kremlin. So Churchill made sure that he personally authorized each and every flight.[7]

But if aerial reconnaissance promised badly needed intelligence, so did the underground operations initiated by Lunn. By now Sir Stewart Menzies, Churchill's trusted wartime head of intelligence, the man who had personally delivered the 'Golden Eggs' on his desk every day, had retired. His successor was Sir John ('Sinbad') Sinclair, a tall, lean and soft-spoken Scot with angular features and the habit of lunching daily on grilled herring and water. He told Churchill about the Vienna tunnels and won his permission to burrow under Berlin. Here, too, discovery by the Soviets could have serious political repercussions. Already fully briefed on bugging techniques being used by the Soviets, Churchill had given MI5 and SIS *carte blanche* to fight back. As a result the Joint Intelligence Committee urgently ordered a programme to develop offensive British eavesdropping techniques.[8] Sinclair and SIS did as instructed.

SIS meets the US Army. Major-General Sir John Sinclair, the SIS chief who authorized the Berlin tunnel, seen here (right) with General Mark Clark, Commander of the Fifth US Army in Italy during the Second World War

Section Y was the equivalent in SIS to CIA's Staff D. Its headquarters was at 2 Carlton Gardens, just off the Mall, which had once been the official residence of Field Marshal Lord Kitchener. At the top of the King George VI steps half-way between Buckingham Palace and Admiralty Arch, its columned entrance faced the former Free French headquarters of General de Gaulle. Behind stood the private residence of the Foreign Secretary. In 1953 its occupant was Sir Anthony Eden, Churchill's impatient and nervous successor-in-waiting. Like his master he was keen to use SIS wherever and whenever he safely could. Section Y, at this epicentre of British power, was ready and eager to deliver.

Inside 2 Carlton Gardens a monumental staircase with gilded bannisters rose from a chandeliered marble entrance hall. Downstairs were public reception rooms. Above was a warren of smaller offices. Below, fronting on the Mall behind solid walls, was the basement where serious work was conducted. This was very special and secret business, closely protected from prying and curious eyes. Here was harvested the intelligence crop flowing in from the Vienna tunnel.

If the set was quintessential Whitehall, then the head of the section came from Ealing Studios central casting. Tom Gimson was a retired army officer whose final post had been as commanding officer of the Irish Guards. In his razor-creased shirt and impeccable pinstripes he kept order over an army of volatile and potentially unruly civilians. 'He was a wonderful manager of men and women,' recalled one colleague, 'his subordinates loved him.' These were the transcribers and translators who sweated day and night to keep pace with the tapes from Vienna being flown in three times a week on a special RAF flight. After the transcribers did their job the results passed on to a second team of a dozen or so army and air force officers with a good knowledge of Russian. They studied the transcribed conversations, extracted intelligence they thought important and compiled a regular intelligence bulletin on the state of the Soviet forces in Austria.

Above: *The statue of King George VI stands guard over the headquarters of SIS's Section Y at 2 Carlton Gardens, just off the Mall. Here transcribers and translators toiled over the tapes from the Vienna tunnel operations*

Left: *2 Carlton Gardens viewed from the Mall. It was here, in the basement, that SIS staff worked unseen on the Vienna tapes*

'The customers got very excited', remembered one of those who was deeply involved. The 'customers' were mostly in War Office intelligence. But the Foreign Office was also an eager consumer. An officer from Gimson's staff kept in regular touch with both of them, strolling across the Mall down Whitehall to deliver material by hand and chat about the results with his opposite numbers in the offices concerned. Sometimes they would ask the transcribers to look out for an especially promising item on the Soviet order of battle or any sudden and threatening moves that might herald an attack on the West.

Barely a decade earlier Churchill had harried Bletchley Park for similar intelligence about Hitler's plans for the invasion of Britain. The turning-point then had come when the code-breakers had cracked a message revealing an order for certain key German units to be stood down. History now repeated itself. Lunn later recalled that one of the most important items in the Vienna harvest was a conversation between two Red Army NCOs discussing which of their units had been earmarked for demobilization. This was 'clear proof', stated Lunn, 'that the Soviets had no intention of launching an attack'.[9]

The job of SIS itself was to run the enterprise. The production team in Carlton Gardens was a remarkable miscellany. Many of them belonged to the so-called 'St Petersburg English', the bilingual descendants of the great British merchant houses that had traded in the former Russian capital before the revolution. Others came from the families of White Russian *émigrés* who had fled the Bolsheviks, mostly middle-aged or elderly and all too happy to use their native tongue to fight the communists while also benefiting from some regular employment. Then there were a number of ex-Polish army officers, mostly former members of the Polish intelligence service fluent in Russian who had been stranded in London after their homeland fell to the communists.

Some were lonely and embittered. As they sat for hours wearing headphones, their work felt lowly, meaningless and tedious. Listening endlessly to tapes of idiomatic yet often highly technical Russian was exhausting and nerve-racking. 'There was plenty of Slav temperament and moodiness about', remembered one witness. Only Gimson's bottomless supply of tact and diplomacy kept affairs running smoothly.

Gimson's large and sunny office had French windows that opened on to a balcony overlooking the Mall. Next door, in a small space converted from a dressing room, sat his personal assistant. This was the formidable Pam Peniakoff. Tall, slim and elegant, she was the English-born widow of Vladimir Peniakoff, a Belgian-born Russian who had led a daring commando group ('Popski's Private Army') in North Africa and Italy against the Germans. Immediately after the war 'Popski' had served in Vienna as British liaison officer with the Red Army, and it was here that he had met and married his wife. She possessed a sharp tongue and an eagle eye, which kept her flock obediently in order.[10]

Then, in the late spring of 1953, the Carlton Gardens team was joined by an exotic new member from SIS. The Vienna material was expanding so rapidly that Gimson was badly in need of a second-in-command. His arrival on the scene was to prove fateful for the entire tunnel project.

7

Agent 'Diomid'

It was a fine Sunday morning in April 1953 when an RAF ambulance plane touched down at Abingdon airfield in Oxfordshire after a short flight from Berlin. Hardly had it taxied up when a Salvation Army chorus began singing the hymn 'Now Thank We All Our God'. Waiting on the runway was a sizeable crowd of journalists, camera-popping photographers, grey-suited civil servants, solemn church dignitaries (including the Archbishop of Canterbury) and tear-stained family members of the six passengers on board.

A lean, bearded man in his thirties, dressed in a heavy thick-spun overcoat, hesitated briefly at the top of the stairs as if wondering whether he should wait for the music to end or descend to the official welcome below. Amid the sea of faces he could see his mother waiting in the crowd. After they had embraced and listened dutifully to formal speeches of welcome, he tumbled into a waiting car and they were driven off to her flat in Reigate.

The first British prisoners from Korea had finally returned home. All were civilians captured during the North Korean invasion of the south who had remarkable tales of hardship and endurance to tell. But none was to prove more fascinating than that of the man with the beard, George Blake. To the British public he was described as the British vice-consul in the South

George Blake being welcomed home by his beaming mother after his repatriation from North Korea, where he had been recruited by the KGB

Korean capital, Seoul. In reality he was an officer in SIS, and the fate of the Berlin tunnel was to hinge on his actions.

Blake had been a catch for SIS. His father was an Egyptian-born Jewish trader and a naturalized Briton named Albert Behar, and his mother was Dutch. He was born in Rotterdam in 1922 and was named after King George V, for whom his father had fought gallantly in the First World War, during which he won both the OBE and Legion of Honour before going on to serve with Field Marshal Douglas Haig's intelligence staff. Educated in the Netherlands until the age of thirteen, George was briefly sent to the English School in Cairo after his father's premature death in 1936. Soon afterwards he returned home and was living in Rotterdam when the Germans invaded.

He joined the Dutch resistance and took part in several dangerous missions, mostly as a courier carrying messages by bicycle. Then, fearing the Gestapo was on his heels, he fled to

Britain along an allied escape line through Belgium, France and Spain. After several months in the Royal Navy, during which he changed his surname to Blake, he worked briefly for SIS's Dutch section before joining the Supreme Headquarters Allied Expeditionary Force (SHAEF) in London planning the invasion of Europe. Now a commissioned officer in the Royal Navy, Blake witnessed the surrender of German forces in north-west Europe at Lüneburg Heath before being transferred to Hamburg for intelligence work. His main task was to collect information for war crimes trials on Admiral Dönitz's submarine service. But he was soon reporting on communist and Soviet activities along the Baltic ports and began to learn Russian.

SIS recruited Blake in 1947. Ironically in the light of what happened later, it was Andrew King who first spotted him in Hamburg during a visit to Germany the year before. On his return to London he mentioned Blake's name to Kenneth Cohen, the overall director of Broadway's European operations. Both he and King were attracted by Blake's proficiency in languages and cosmopolitan background. People like him were hard to find in Britain and SIS badly needed new blood for its Cold War projects.

As a start Blake was sent to Downing College, Cambridge, for an intensive Russian language course. Then, in 1949, he joined the small British legation in Seoul. A year later North Korea invaded and within four days had captured the capital. Blake, along with other legation members, was sent to a POW camp, first in the north and then across the Yalu River into Chinese Manchuria. Life there was marked by deprivation, starvation and disease, with numerous attempts at brainwashing. When the survivors arrived in Abingdon they were received as national heroes.

Blake was no exception. After a routine debriefing to check that no SIS ciphers or documents had fallen into North Korean hands, he was told to report to the Far Eastern section in Broadway. Here he found himself treated as a celebrity by the young female secretaries. But others were also starstruck. John

Wyke, fresh from his Vienna tunnelling exploits, was typical in his admiration. Blake had survived real horrors, felt Wyke, and his reputation in Broadway rode high.[1] Even the austere Sir John Sinclair, 'C' himself, was warm and sympathetic. After a brief chat about Blake's hardships in Korea, he suggested he take a few weeks' leave while they found him a posting at home.

Blake bought a car and took his mother and his newly wed sister and her husband on a holiday to Spain. On the way back he and his mother spent a week in Rotterdam with an aunt. In the summer, ever the family man and loving brother, he took his eldest sister for a holiday to France. By September he was installed with 'Y' section in Carlton Gardens. Soon after that he began to date the youngest of Pam Peniakoff's brood, a tall and dark-haired secretary some ten years younger than himself, named Gillian Allan. They married a year later in St Peter's, North Audley Street, a fashionable church in London's West End. It was the sort of marriage SIS welcomed. Not only was Blake marrying a wife inside the service. Gillian's father, a colonel, also worked for the firm. As Blake wryly noted, 'it kept everything nicely in the family.'[2]

★

But what nobody in SIS knew was that Blake had already joined another intelligence family. During his imprisonment in Manchuria he had volunteered his services to the KGB. Some observers have claimed this was pure expediency, but Blake himself has always insisted it was a genuine conversion to communism. It seems to have been a bit of both. He possessed a strong ascetic streak and at one point seriously considered becoming a minister in the Dutch Reformed Church. His cousin Henri Curiel became a leader of the Egyptian communist party. With his Dutch–Jewish background and slightly accented English, he sometimes felt, or was made to feel, an outsider in SIS. He was favourably influenced by learning about Russian life and literature at Cambridge and apparently shocked by the brutality of the South Korean regime of Syngman Rhee.

The Western-backed dictator ruled over a feudal state with a wretched and impoverished peasantry and a police force that reminded Blake of the Gestapo. Communist partisans in the hills harassed government forces. 'They seemed to me', claimed Blake later, 'not unlike our own resistance fighters in Europe during the war.' This smacks of an *ex post facto* justification, for there was plenty to suggest that the North Koreans and the Chinese were even more Gestapo-like than their opponents.

Whatever his motivation, one night in the autumn of 1951 Blake managed to slip a note to a prison guard. Writing in Russian and addressing himself to the Soviet embassy in Pyongyang, he requested a meeting as he had something important to communicate. Six weeks later the prisoners were summoned, one by one, for an interview. When Blake took his turn he found a Russian officer behind the desk. A big, burly man with a pale complexion, he wore no socks and was shaven-headed. He reminded Blake of the film actor Erich von Stroheim. This was the KGB head in Manchuria, where Mao Tse-tung had granted them a base. He asked Blake what he had to tell, listened carefully, asked Blake to write it all down in English, then questioned him about his early life and work with SIS. Blake had crossed the Rubicon.

It was a good eighteen months before he first met his first Russian control in the West. The meeting took place in April 1953 at the heavily guarded and isolated frontier post of Otpor, where the Trans-Siberian Express from Peking to Moscow crossed the Chinese–Soviet border. Despite Mao's victory and a Soviet–Chinese friendship treaty, it was disfigured by minefields, electrified wires, strips of raked sand and watch-towers. Blake and his fellow prisoners were on their way home. One by one they were summoned from the train to show travel documents and fill in forms. When it came to Blake's turn he was led into an inner office. A thick-set man aged about fifty, who spoke English well but with a marked Slav accent, was waiting. He did not introduce himself but said simply that in future he and Blake would be working together.

Nikolai Borisovich Rodin, also known as Korovin, was a stereotypical and arrogant apparatchik. He was the main London KGB *rezident* and had made the journey across Russia specifically to meet the new recruit. Blake found him cold – 'too much of the iron fist in the velvet glove' – but he admired the skill and professionalism of this skilled agent-handler.[3] Rodin came quickly to the point. How would they make contact once Blake was back in Britain? Blake immediately suggested the Netherlands, a place where he felt at home and where his instincts would tell him quickly if anything was amiss. They agreed on a date in July, with several alternatives if anything went wrong. Each would carry a copy of the previous day's *Nieuwe Rotterdamse Courant* as a sign that all was well. The KGB code-named Blake 'Diomid'. Literally translated, the word means 'Diamond' but it also conveys the sense of 'valuable', 'clear' and 'rare', attributes that testify to the high value the KGB already placed on their British mole.

Blake's trip with his mother to Rotterdam that summer provided the perfect opportunity for a meeting in The Hague. The rendezvous was a small square built around a garden near the end of the Laan van Meerdervoort, the longest avenue in the city. Here, among children playing and adults taking gentle strolls in the summer air, they would meet. Blake found a pretext to slip away from his mother, drove his car to The Hague and parked. It was a fine day. Walking slowly and drawing on his SIS trade-craft, he checked he was not being followed. His copy of the newspaper was in his right hand. There on a bench, alone, was Rodin, also with his newspaper. Blake sat down. What had happened since his return to Britain, asked his control. 'Diomid' told him about his new appointment as Gimson's deputy in Section Y and the two men agreed to meet next in London. Before they finished Blake drew Rodin's attention to the headlines in their papers. Lavrenti Beria, the dreaded head of the KGB and Stalin's former henchman, had been arrested in Moscow and denounced as a British agent. Rodin looked embarrassed. Blake should not take this literally, he said, he was safe. With a nervous laugh Blake assured Rodin that he had no doubt about that. After twenty minutes they parted. Blake again made certain he was not being tailed and drove back to Rotterdam on side roads.

In fact, the newly recruited mole had had an extremely close shave. Rodin was being kept under close surveillance. An MI5 team of watchers had followed him from the Soviet embassy all the way to the Netherlands, where they handed over the task to their Dutch counterparts, but Rodin had given them the slip. They picked him up again only after he returned to the ferry to sail back to Britain. Both MI5 and the Dutch spent a lot of time trying to guess the reason for his trip but failed to come up with an answer.

Meanwhile the man who could have told them was falling into his daily routine at Carlton Gardens, joking with the secretaries, collecting material from the wearied transcribers, earnestly discussing its Vienna content with Gimson, liaising with his insatiable customers in the War Office and returning each evening to his mother's convenient new flat in Baron's Court. The most important part of his life lay in his clandestine meetings after hours with his Soviet contact. Adding a special *frisson* to this mission was the endless office gossip about treachery. The defections of Burgess and Maclean to Moscow just two years earlier had sent shock waves through Whitehall. Only a fortnight after his arrival in Carlton Gardens Blake received an urgent message from his Broadway headquarters. Melinda Maclean, left behind by her defecting husband, had disappeared from Switzerland, where she had been staying with her mother. It was suspected, correctly, that she had joined her husband in Moscow. Perhaps she had fled across the border through Soviet-occupied Austria, in which case, Blake was ordered, he should instruct the transcribers to look for evidence in the Vienna telephone material they were processing. Nothing came of it, but the episode brought it all uncomfortably close. Mention of Maclean and Burgess always sent a chill down Blake's spine.

By now Moscow had decided that having Rodin as his control was far too risky for such a priceless asset as 'Diomid'. Rodin was too well known to MI5 and their surveillance of the KGB *rezident* might well lead to disaster. Instead they sent an officer so far unknown to British counter-intelligence, Sergei Aleksandrovich Kondrashev. He was young and had only recently joined the foreign intelligence directorate, although he had plenty of surveillance and counter-surveillance experience. 'One day I was called in and told I would soon be posted to London to work with a very important source', recalled Kondrashev in a newspaper interview many years later. 'That's all I was told. I had never been to London and was given several months to prepare. I studied maps of the city, became acquainted with British methods of surveillance, and was then handed Blake's personal file, which I studied very carefully.'[4]

In October 1953 Kondrashev arrived in London under the cover of First Secretary for Cultural Relations. Here he busied himself with such formal tasks as arranging a tour of Britain for the celebrated Russian violinist David Oistrakh and purchasing tickets for visiting Soviet VIPs to attend sports events. To mix in with his surroundings – and undoubtedly influenced by his reading about Britain – he even wore grey flannel trousers and a blue blazer. But secretly he began plotting his contact with Blake. Even within the KGB *residenz* he kept this knowledge to himself. Only he knew the real identity or position of 'Diomid'. Handling him was not easy, either, because of Moscow's close interest and interference. 'The pressure from Moscow was enormous', he remembered, 'and I was pretty tense . . . There was no room for mistakes.'[5]

Soon afterwards Blake and Kondrashev met for the first of many clandestine encounters. 'I left my office as usual after six', recalled Blake, 'and walked in a leisurely way through Soho to Oxford Street.' Here he stopped in a café for a cup of tea, to check if he was being followed. Reassured he was not, he walked back to Charing Cross underground station and boarded a Northern Line train heading north. At the next station he jumped off just as the doors were closing, waited for the next two trains to pass, then boarded the third. At Belsize Park he waited again until the doors were about to close, then leaped off. The coast was clear and he set off by foot for the rendezvous he had agreed on three months earlier with Rodin in The Hague. As a sign that all was well he carried a newspaper in his left hand. On a quiet residential street, at the spot agreed, a man suddenly loomed out of the fog. 'In his grey, soft felt hat and smart grey raincoat he seemed almost part of the fog', Blake recalled. The man, too, was carrying a newspaper in his left hand. It was Kondrashev.

Later on, in his published memoirs, Blake would claim that his contact in Belsize Park was Rodin, the man he had first met on the Sino-Soviet border. But this was a deliberate deception. At the time Blake was writing his book in Moscow the Soviet Union, and more importantly the KGB, still existed and

George Blake (bearded), next to his former KGB controller, Sergei Kondrashev (in uniform), addresses KGB officers in Moscow a year before the collapse of the Soviet Union

Kondrashev was a member of the Soviet delegation in talks on human rights at a conference in Madrid. The KGB told Blake they did not wish to embarrass their political masters by having Kondrashev's role publicly revealed at such a sensitive time.[6]

★

At this first meeting Blake handed over to Kondrashev a written list of top secret technical operations being carried out by Section Y against the Soviet Union and explained them in more detail. They involved both telephone taps and the microphone buggings of Eastern bloc embassies in London now fully under way with Peter Wright and MI5. But by far the most important, he stressed, were the Vienna tunnel operations inaugurated by Lunn. He also discussed his need for a camera to process the hundreds of files. The two men then agreed on their next meeting place and fall-back arrangements. 'I was impressed by [Blake's] calmness and self-possessed manner', recalled Kondrashev, 'I can't ever recall seeing him under real stress.'

Three weeks later the KGB officer slipped Blake a Minox camera, which from now on he took into Carlton Gardens concealed in the back pocket of his trousers. He was not a natural photographer and, given his natural haste for fear of being caught, it was quite a while before he delivered anything of much use to Kondrashev. But gradually he improved his technique. The two men met every three or four weeks from now on, close to some underground stop and only after carefully following counter-surveillance techniques. At his third or fourth meeting Blake gave Kondrashev a copy of the most recent Carlton Gardens intelligence bulletin on Soviet forces in Austria. This was based on the Vienna operation. Some thirty or forty pages long, and classified 'Most Secret', it went regularly to the main SIS customers in Whitehall as well as to the Americans in Washington. From now on, Blake made sure that it also went to Moscow.

Then, just before Christmas, he stumbled on a goldmine of new and dramatic information to pass on to the KGB.

8

Operation Stopwatch / Gold

By now the CIA's cable-tapping plans were in top gear. Bill Harvey arrived in Berlin in the autumn of 1952 to take personal charge. He was nominally head of the Berlin base but his real assignment, known only to himself, Rowlett and one or two others in Washington, was to spearhead the tunnel operation; from now on the tiny handful of those Americans in the know would nickname the project 'Harvey's Hole'. Already Walter O'Brien's work running his agents in East Berlin and the GDR had grown considerably. To help him, Harvey brought in Hugh Montgomery, a former Office of Strategic Services counter-intelligence expert.

Working in Austria and Germany with Richard Helms, Montgomery was a linguist who had returned to Harvard after the war to finish his degree and take up teaching. Bored by academic life, he joined the CIA in 1952 but knew nothing about the tunnel when he arrived in Berlin. Instead, Harvey asked him to work with O'Brien on expanding coverage of the East German cable system by debriefing refugees, who were arriving daily. He also learned about the 'Numbers Girl'. He remembered that she wrote the crucial information down on small old-fashioned cards. 'Our asset – her former boss who'd come over to the West – smuggled them out in his underwear', he recalled later. 'They arrived a bit crumpled and dirty and we had to smooth them out. But he never gave us her name. We worked it out from an organizational chart. "There's one name I'll make sure I forget" I said. And I have . . .'[1]

Eventually Harvey briefed both Montgomery and O'Brien on the tunnel, although by then O'Brien's work was mainly done and he soon moved on, eventually to become head of the agency's East European division. Joining Montgomery in Berlin as part of the core tunnel team were the laconic Charlie Arnold, a taciturn veteran of the Vienna operations whom Harvey instantly nicknamed 'The Great Stoneface', another technical expert, named Vyrl Lichleiter, and F. E. (Eddie) Kindell as the on-site chief of communications. Together with Truscott and 'Fleetfoot' in Frankfurt these were the only CIA men in Germany who knew about the tunnel. Harvey drilled the need for security firmly into Montgomery. 'Bill didn't want me going to Rudow more than necessary,' he recalled, 'so I used to go at night in someone else's car or in an army jeep.'

Security was just as tight in Washington, with everything kept on a strict need-to-know basis. Frank Rowlett moved into CIA headquarters to give overall direction. To keep in touch he frequently flew across the Atlantic for verbal briefings at the CIA offices in Frankfurt. His years of working on cipher machines had made him an incredibly fast typist. Now, bending over his typewriter, he would rattle out extensive notes as the team described their progress.[2]

The taps could be done, that was clear. But what next? Harvey's team narrowed the choice to two possible sites in Berlin. Both lay in the American sector. Eventually they opted for Rudow. Here the water table was relatively low, which meant that the tunnel could be constructed without the complication and expense of watertight construction and locks. The site was also conveniently close to the Soviet sector border, and plenty of vacant land was available. The Rudow taps also held out the promise of a rich and exciting harvest of intelligence. Here lay three cables, all carrying top-grade intelligence material.

But there was a problem. The tunnel, more than two-thirds

of which would lie beneath the Soviet sector of the city, would be 1,800 feet long and produce about 3,000 tons of the sandy soil on which Berlin was built. 'Where do we put it?' was a question that haunted the team for weeks. Eventually, exhausted by endless discussions, one of them facetiously suggested they dig a hole and put the soil in it.

Mad though it sounded, the idea was perfect. Three large warehouses would be built at the site of the tunnel's entrance. They would be disguised as emergency equipment dispersal units for the American occupation forces in the city. Plenty such buildings had sprung up since 1945. While the Soviets would doubtless be interested, they would have no idea of what was happening underground. One of the warehouses would be built with an exceptionally deep basement to store the soil from the tunnel. In each of the buildings a highly trained and hand-picked team of two officers and sixteen enlisted men would work on digging the tunnel and handling the necessary equipment.

Harvey's team estimated that from the beginning of construction to the placing of the first tap would take nine months. The cost, not including the building of the warehouses, would be in the region of $500,000. This proved hopelessly optimistic. In the end the bill came to over $6 million. It might have seemed possible to include this in occupation costs, which were picked up by the West German taxpayers. But if the idea ever occurred to anyone it was promptly quashed as far too risky. The amounts were huge and not easily hidden. Besides, West Germany was deeply penetrated by Soviet and Stasi intelligence. The entire operation from top to bottom had to be hermetically sealed from the Germans.

The target date for completion was the late summer of 1954. At every stage and every level the success of the plan would rest on maximum security. Knowledge of the operation would be kept watertight. Only those specially initiated into its secret would know about it. And a special system would be put in place to deal with all communications about the project.

By August 1953 the outline plan was in place. Rowlett flew

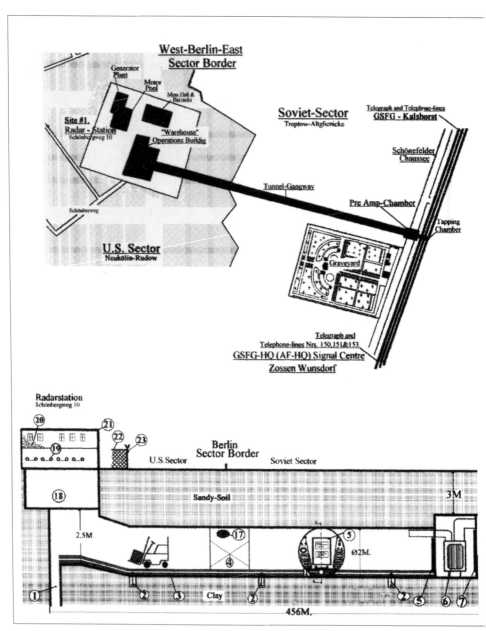

Operation Stopwatch/Gold: (top left) aerial diagram of the Berlin tunnel operation; (top right) map showing Red Army dispositions in East Germany; (bottom) cross-section plan of the tunnel

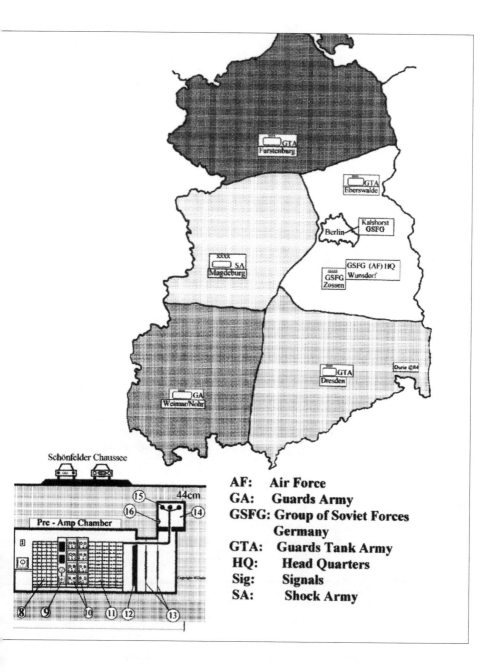

AF: Air Force
GA: Guards Army
GSFG: Group of Soviet Forces
       Germany
GTA: Guards Tank Army
HQ: Head Quarters
Sig: Signals
SA: Shock Army

out to the CIA base in Frankfurt for a last review with Harvey.
Truscott and his top aides were present and, after giving it his
blessing, the head of CIA Germany decided that the time had
finally come to take it to the very top for final approval: to the
Director of the CIA himself.

With his briar pipe, rimless glasses and white moustache, the
dumpy Allen Dulles was an avuncular figure. Kenneth Strong,
Eisenhower's British wartime intelligence chief and now chairman of Britain's Joint Intelligence Bureau, recalled that he had
an 'infectious, gusty laugh, which always seemed to enter a room
with him'. He had a ready smile and relaxed, informal, manner,
but the appearance was deceptive. Behind the charm lay a tough,
decisive and often devious mind fascinated by what he himself
termed 'the craft of intelligence'. 'He was a hale fellow', recalled
the novelist Louis Auchinloss, who had once worked with
Dulles as a young lawyer, 'but his laugh was humourless.'
Although he had sat in the Director's chair only since Eisenhower's inauguration that January, to many it seemed he had long
been running things behind the scenes as the agency's deputy
director.

Dulles was a hardened veteran of America's intelligence wars.
Chief of the OSS mission in wartime Switzerland, he made his
name running a network of spies throughout Europe. Berne was
a hothouse for espionage. 'We all ate at the Bellevue Hotel',
recalled one of his staff. 'At one table would be all the Polish
agents, at another the Nazi agents, another would have all the
British, another all the Americans.'[3] Afterwards Dulles had
flown into the ruins of post-war Berlin to establish its base there
before rapidly climbing the CIA ladder. He had little time for
bureaucracy and loved covert action. He was, said Strong, 'the
last of the great Intelligence officers whose stock-in-trade consisted of secrets and mysteries . . . [and] . . . the last great
Romantic of Intelligence'. Dulles delighted in his reputation as
a master spy and insisted that proposals for operations be submitted to him on a single sheet of paper. 'Okay, let's give it a try',
he would say to those which met his approval.[4]

Beside him Dulles had the new Secretary of State, his brother John Foster Dulles, a convinced Cold War hardliner. This was useful. Far more valuable, however, was the presence of Eisenhower in the White House. Unlike Truman, Eisenhower had experienced at first hand the value of military intelligence. He was also committed in principle to covert action as an alternative to costly military action. 'Some of our traditional ideas of international sportsmanship', he wrote privately, 'are scarcely applicable in the morass in which the world now founders.'[5] During his eight years in the White House the scope of CIA activities increased dramatically. But the President was always careful to keep the paper trail with the White House to the absolute minimum. He preferred to give verbal approval.

Dulles, confident of Eisenhower's consent, quickly agreed with Truscott that the intelligence potential of the tunnel justified the inherent risk and financial cost. Crucial to its success, stressed Truscott, would be maintaining the highest possible degree of security. Only individuals who could make a direct contribution should know. The project would also require support from key Washington players beyond the CIA, especially in the Pentagon and the White House. Dulles assured him on all these points. He also emphasized that as little as possible should be written down, although for his own personal interest he would like to see a more detailed plan.[6]

★

'Precisely at what point the idea of a tunnel for the purpose of tapping the target cables began to come into focus cannot be pinpointed', records the CIA's internal history of the project. Nor does it reveal any specific date when the CIA and SIS began to work together on the operation. The Americans had begun their cable reconnaisance work in Berlin independently of the British. But after O'Brien's successes in targeting spots, Rowlett and Helms decided they should bring in SIS. 'We had everything about the East German cable system and we guessed they'd be doing something of the sort', recalled O'Brien. So he and

'Fleetfoot' flew to London and laid out what they had got to SIS. From then on it was a joint operation. The British possessed vital expertise lacked by the CIA, as Vienna had proved. 'It couldn't possibly have been done without the British', Montgomery said later. 'We simply didn't have the technical expertise to carry out the tap.'

It was certainly no coincidence that in mid-1953 Peter Lunn arrived in Berlin as the SIS head of station. Based in its offices by the Olympic Stadium were about thirty officers and twice as many support staff: technicians, secretaries, signals experts and drivers. Security and counter-surveillance techniques were intense. Officers drove around the city for meetings with agents in battered old Volkswagens. Technical wizards developed a James Bond device to fool KGB watchers. After leaving the compound the driver could operate a switch on the dashboard and the licence plates would swivel round to display a completely different number.

Such tricks had a venerable wartime pedigree. Lunn's second-in-command was J.W. (Jimmy) Munn, an SOE veteran who had run its famous training school for agents at Beaulieu before heading its 'Massingham' operation in North Africa. After that he had joined the post-war exodus out of SOE into SIS, and for a while run its training school at Gosport, close to Portsmouth, a walled encampment originally built by Henry VIII.

Lunn's reputation had been immeasurably enhanced by his success in Vienna. His next posting, Berne, was an essential career stepping-stone as well as networking centre. It was here, at about the same time, that the novelist John Le Carré, then simply David Cornwell, cut his intelligence teeth working for the local SIS. From Berne, Allen Dulles had built his wartime networks into Germany and strategically positioned himself for his later rise to the top of the CIA. Here too, in the city's ancient, arcaded streets, Andrew King had spent much of the war and come to know Dulles well. Once a week he and the future CIA Director exchanged items of intelligence over breakfast. This personal contact proved valuable when King later had to make regular trips to Washington to discuss progress on the tunnel. Lunn's predecessor in Berne was a fellow high-flyer in the service, Nicholas Elliott, the officer chosen several years later to confront Kim Philby with the irrefutable evidence of his treachery. But immediately on leaving Berne, Elliott was appointed to a high-level position in the Broadway headquarters as Controller of Production Research. Here, during the crucial period of the tunnel's life between 1953 and 1956, Andrew King served as his deputy and head of the London station.

Lunn enjoyed himself in Berne, and Switzerland was his second home. During one of his many skiing outings into the mountains a friend high up in City of London financial circles came out to visit, bringing his ten-year-old son. Early one morning the three of them took a lift to a snow-covered peak to watch the rising sun. As its rays poetically turned the snow to pink, the boy turned to his father. 'Look, daddy,' he cried, 'it's the colour of the *Financial Times*.' It was a story that Lunn relished, a happy memento of almost carefree times.

Berlin offered a radically different challenge. British intelligence remained desperate for front-line information about the Red Army. Fanning out from Potsdam to all quarters of the Soviet zone, specialist units of Brixmis – officially, the British Commander-in-Chief's Mission to the Soviet Forces of Occupation in Germany – strenuously recorded whatever they could see about the Soviet order of battle. Harried by the Soviets and frequently threatened by the East German police, they drove thousands of miles in their search for evidence about Soviet military dispositions. Efforts peaked at about the time Lunn arrived in Berlin, when a Brixmis team managed to reconstruct an entire Soviet battle exercise held in East Germany. The mission worked closely with its American equivalent and its targets were closely co-ordinated with SIS.[7]

But however successful, Brixmis by definition could only record what they could see, namely military hardware. Soviet intentions were intangible and required other means, such as the tunnel. Lunn immediately established a special technical section to repeat the Vienna success. To run it, he brought in the dapper John Wyke and housed him in a unit some way away from the Olympic Stadium offices, from which he kept his distance. Some of his time he spent out at Gatow airfield, practising digging techniques in the sandy Berlin soil.

Inevitably, Lunn was soon in talks with Bill Harvey. Poles apart in personality, they none the less respected each other's talents and they had one thing in common: a fierce determination to outwit the Soviets. Lunn's own investigations led independently to the conclusion that the Rudow site was the best. But as it lay inside the American sector he and Harvey would have to work together. The CIA would bear most of the cost – always an advantage in joint Anglo-American intelligence operations – and Harvey would find the bulk of the labour for the warehouse and tunnel construction and take care of the host of logistical and security problems.

On the strict 'need-to-know' security basis laid down for the project, SIS would not be involved for most of this phase, although its advice would be sought on engineering aspects of the operation. But only Lunn and SIS could provide the crucial item for the final phase of the plan: the expertise needed for placing the tap itself. This was the most critical part of the oper-ation. It was a particularly acute hazard because the cables that had been targeted lay only 28 inches beneath the surface. To make matters worse, they ran directly beneath a major and heavily travelled highway, the Schönefelder Chaussee. A vertical shaft would have to be dug from the tunnel up to the cables without causing the sandy ground to collapse or the tap itself to be detected.

The only man with the proven skill to do this was Wyke, assisted again by John Taylor and his post office phone-tapping team from London. 'Experience from similar operations else-where', noted Harvey in his brief for Truscott, indicated that the job, despite all its technical and engineering problems, could be done. For SIS the Vienna tunnels had paid off. They not only delivered valuable intelligence on the Soviets but also presented an irresistible claim for the Berlin tunnel to be a joint Anglo-American operation. Without Vienna there would never have been a Berlin tunnel.

SIS code-named it Stopwatch; the CIA called it Gold. Ideally, code names should be chosen randomly to conceal, not reveal, the target and value of the operation. (The Soviets were hardly more careful: they had, after all, given Blake the code name 'Diamond'.) But perhaps the temptation was impossible to avoid. If successful, the tunnel would produce prime intelligence, analagous to the Magic delivered by Rowlett's brilliant code-breaking offensive against the Japanese during the Second World War. For SIS, closer to the Cold War front line in Europe, the tunnel might deliver precious warning of Soviet attack, a countdown to Armageddon that could be measured with stopwatch precision.

Even as Dulles was reviewing the plan in Washington, Churchill was again pressing hard for intelligence on Soviet strength. 'What', he impatiently asked his Minister of Defence in October 1953, 'is the latest statement of the relative strengths in Europe of the Russian and satellite forces compared to the Nato forces?' Demands such as these acted as a constant spur to action. SIS, as always, was keen to demonstrate that it could deliver the goods.[8]

9

'Kilts Up, Bill!'

Known to Berliners as 'The Sleeping Beauty Castle', the four-power Allied Control Council Headquarters was a vast deserted building of over 500 rooms that had stood empty since the Soviet commander in Germany, Marshal Sokolovsky, stormed out of it on the eve of the Berlin blockade. Under Hitler it had housed the Nazis' notorious 'People's Court', where the presiding judge, Roland Freisler, had sentenced hundreds of victims to death. Shortly after the Bermuda summit between Churchill and Eisenhower in late 1953, an army of painters, electricians and carpenters descended on the building to spruce it up for a foreign ministers' summit. The meeting was widely seen as crucial to European and world peace. Its agenda was the future of Germany.

Moscow, Washington and London still officially regarded the division of the country as temporary. As 1954 opened, talk of reunification was in the air. Gestures from Moscow hinted at a softer and more conciliatory line. Stalin's death the year before had raised hopes of *détente*. The Soviets had even agreed to repatriate thousands of German prisoners of war held in the gulags of Siberia since their capture on the Eastern Front. 'They came', wrote Alistair Horne, the *Daily Telegraph* correspondent in the city, who watched some 10,000 survivors straggle over the inter-zonal border, 'in bedraggled batches of about a thousand a time.'

Many were survivors of Stalingrad, pathetic creatures enfeebled by a decade of forced labour. They were instantly besieged by thousands of distraught women hoping against hope to find their men still alive.[1]

But the majority quickly learned they were widows. Hopes for the summit also died. East and West spoke of reunification, but each on terms that were unacceptable to the other. The post-Stalin thaw was but a brief interlude. Three weeks after its opening the summit limped to its end. Outside the temperature was -30°C. Confrontation within was just as frigid. On his flight back to Washington the American Secretary of State, John Foster Dulles, touched down outside Bonn to confer with Konrad Adenauer. Now, Dulles told him, Washington would double the pace of rearmament of West Germany. Nineteen fifty-four, which the CIA had predicted ever since Korea would be the year of 'maximum danger' for global war, had started on an ominous note.

It continued that way. Within weeks the Americans exploded their first hydrogen bomb, dropped by plane 10,000 feet above Bikini Atoll in the Pacific, creating a fireball four miles wide. The explosion, reported the *Daily Telegraph*, 'was the most stupendous ever released on earth'. Before the year was out the United States and Canada had also put in place the Distant Early Warning (DEW) line, a chain of radar stations across the Arctic to scan the skies for incoming Soviet bombers. Across America a campaign was launched to build fall-out shelters in all major cities.

In London, Churchill also feared Armageddon. Even before the Berlin summit collapsed he was bombarding his Minister of Defence and wartime friend, Field Marshal Earl Alexander of Tunis, with anxious queries. 'Could you let me have the best layout your Intelligence permits of the Soviet dispositions and deployment in relation to the Western Front (a) now (b) one year ago (c) two years ago?', he demanded early in February. 'I have seen it stated that there have been large-scale movements of their forces both eastward and northward. I am thinking about the chances of an Alert for ground attack caused by necessary hostile concentration.' Alexander was long used to Churchill's alarms. After consulting the Joint Intelligence Committee he reassured him there had been no significant changes in Red Army strength or dispositions.

The Foreign Office also reminded Churchill that they would almost certainly obtain advance warning of any attack. Their explanation was simple. Moscow was vastly inferior to the United States in atomic weapons and would only launch a sudden attack alongside a rapid advance of its massive ground forces into Western Europe. No such attack could happen without Western intelligence being aware. Churchill believed this period would give a breathing-space for the West both to deter the Soviets and to place its own forces on the alert. The Foreign Office also took care to play a card they knew would impress the Prime Minister. 'The friends', they told him, using the Whitehall euphemism for SIS, 'concur in it.' [2]

'The friends' indeed had every reason for confidence about an early warning. For even as the Berlin summit came and went they were deeply involved in detailed planning discussions with the CIA in London about the tunnel.

★

Britain was at last emerging from the long drab years of post-war austerity. The national mood was buoyant. The Korean armistice was signed. England under Len Hutton won back the Ashes from Australia. The footballing 'Wizard of Dribble' Stanley Matthews won his first cup winner's medal at the age of thirty-eight. The new royal yacht, *Britannia*, was launched on Clydebank, and for the first time since 1940 white bread returned for sale in the shops. Six months earlier the British climbing team led by John Hunt had been the first to conquer Mount Everest. Photographs of the Union Jack fluttering from its summit had been splashed across newspapers and television screens, an event that happily coincided with the largest outpouring of national celebration since Victory in Europe, the coronation of Britain's new young monarch, Queen Elizabeth II. Watched by millions on their new black and white television sets, it provided a pageant of splendour and ritual that brought optimism after years of depression and war: the dawn, newspapers declared, of a new Elizabethan age. Ironically, the year also saw the début of James Bond with the publication of Ian Fleming's first novel, *Casino Royale*. Even the newly released George Blake shared in the mood. In the garden of Carlton Gardens a special stand had been erected and he was invited to join the upper echelons of SIS for a front seat view of the coronation procession down the Mall. Afterwards he joined the SIS top brass in a cheerful champagne celebration.

Bolstering national morale was the knowledge that Churchill was once again flying the flag for Great Britain on the world stage. He had also been made a Knight of the Garter and to cap it had won the Nobel Prize for Literature. His top-level summit in Bermuda with his old wartime companion-in-arms Eisenhower reassured the nation that the 'special relationship' between London and Washington, forged in the fire of Hitler's war, was again secure.

Certainly, this is what a small group of men sitting around a table hardly a stone's throw from Churchill's official residence at 10 Downing Street took for granted. In fact, they embodied the core of the London–Washington intelligence link. Five of them were from the CIA. The other nine represented Britain's SIS. Their meeting place was 2 Carlton Gardens, the offices of Tom Gimson's Section Y.

The date was 15 December 1953. The Berlin summit had yet to open, but these were men already preparing for its failure. Like most intelligence professionals they were insurance salesmen at heart, preparing for the worst. Churchill may have been pinning his hopes for peace on the summit's outcome, but the thoughts of those around the table at Carlton Gardens were dominated by his nightmare of war. Thirty Red Army divisions were based in Germany. Why were they there? What did the Kremlin have in mind? What exactly was the shape and state of Soviet forces, and where and how would they move? The Iron Curtain was now virtually impenetrable. Both the CIA and SIS were finding it virtually impossible to run agents behind enemy lines.

Yet there were crucial clues. In 1954 British intelligence experts were broadly confident that Moscow did not wish deliberately to start a war. The West enjoyed enormous superiority in atomic bombs and – in the pre-missile era – the aircraft needed to deliver them. Moreover, Soviet air defences were noticeably weak. Only when it had eliminated these shortcomings would the Soviet Union think of starting a war. This meant that Western intelligence should target five main areas, or 'indicators', to determine if and when the balance had shifted. These were: Soviet heavy bomber production, where at least 200 aircraft capable of carrying out inter-continental atomic strikes against the United States would be needed; Soviet medium bomber production; the possession by Moscow of at least 1,000 all-weather fighters for defence ('At present', noted a Top Secret intelligence report of the time, 'there is no such evidence that such an aircraft has flown'); advances in Soviet radar technology; and the standards of training for Soviet heavy and medium bomber crew which, the same report noted, was presently low.

Beyond these five main target areas close watch should also obviously be kept on other branches of the Soviet armed forces, such as the navy, army, and tactical air force. This was a global intelligence agenda. But Germany was literally on the Cold War front line and here the richest crop of high-grade intelligence was vital. Whatever happened politically in Germany, declared the Joint Services Intelligence Group for Germany in 1954, 'the present requirement is for a considerable increase'.[3]

There was a significant additional reason for good intelligence from Germany besides reporting on the Red Army. Conflicting estimates of Soviet intentions could create dangerous disagreements between Washington and London. On the whole, the Americans were more alarmist than their transatlantic cousins. In 1951 Britain's Director of Naval Intelligence, Vice-Admiral Eric Longley-Cooke, a veteran of numerous inter-allied intelligence meetings, visited Washington. He came to the disturbing conclusion that the Americans were convinced that all-out war with Moscow was not only inevitable but imminent, and that they were shaping their intelligence to 'fit in' with this prejudged conclusion. 'There is a strong tendency in [American] military circles', noted Longley-Cooke, 'to "fix" the zero date for war.'[4]

So potentially ruinous to allied relations was his report that all copies were destroyed but one, which was kept in the Prime Minister's office. Attlee did little with it. But when Churchill became Prime Minister he ordered it resurrected for his personal consumption.[5] Critics have frequently accused Churchill of being some sort of 'lapdog' to Washington. An enthusiast of the special relationship he certainly was. But his visits to see Truman and Eisenhower convinced him that much of what Longley-Cooke said was true. It was all the more vital, therefore, to make sure that London and Washington shared the same clear and accurate view of Soviet intentions.

Partly under his prodding American and British evaluations had come closer together, but mutterings in Washington could still be heard about British 'appeasement'. The Joint Intelligence Committee insisted that a combined appreciation of the Soviet threat based on 'factual intelligence' was badly needed. Fears lingered of dangerous allied discord. Churchill was determined to avoid it. A combined operation such as Stopwatch/Gold, producing hard intelligence that would be equally shared, could serve as a useful harmonizer of allied responses to the Red Army threat.

Stopwatch/Gold offered the promise of unearthing many of the crucial clues being sought by the West. That is why the CIA and SIS men were there that December. They had in front of them the blueprint for the Berlin tunnel. The London meeting had been called to reach preliminary agreement on the major issues, including the Anglo-American division of labour. Heading the small CIA team was Frank Rowlett, accompanied by his personal assistant, William Wheeler. Carl Nelson was there, and so was Vyrl Lichleiter from Berlin. The larger SIS team was headed by Stewart Mackenzie, a future controller of operations for western hemisphere operations, and included the head of Section Y, Tom Gimson, and George Young, an ebullient ex-journalist from the *Glasgow Herald* and now Broadway's Director of Requirements. Young, who determined SIS targets, enjoyed a reputation as one of the so-called 'robber barons' running SIS at the height of the Cold War.

Inside George Young burned the fires of an almost missionary zeal that easily matched Allen Dulles's robust approach to Cold War priorities. 'It is the spy who has been called upon to remedy the situation created by the deficiencies of ministers, diplomats, generals, and priests', he declared to fellow officers during a barnstorming inspection visit to Lunn's Berlin station. 'We spies live closer to the realities and hard facts of international relations than other practitioners of government . . . these days the spy finds himself the main guardian of intellectual integrity.'[6] Backing up Young's rhetoric were both Colonel Balmain and Dollis Hill's John Taylor. With the Vienna tunnel securely tucked under their belts, they were present to discuss technical details with the CIA boffins. But the main issues to be decided involved the processing of the intelligence.

From experience in Vienna it was obvious to all those round the table that a huge team of experts would be needed to process the Berlin material. The three Soviet cables being targeted under the Schönefelder Chaussee contained at least 81 speech circuits, producing a total of 162 two-and-a-half hour reels of tape each day. Each circuit needed a transcriber. Along with collators, cardists, signals experts and typists, the minimum number of people involved would be 158.

Should the CIA and SIS have two separate teams, or just one integrated team? Should they be based in London, Washington or Berlin itself? How should its members be chosen? In recruiting for the Vienna operation Section Y had sought out native Russian- or Slav-speakers in the belief that they could handle spoken material best: hence the recruitment of Pam Peniakoff's small civilian army of Poles and White Russians. But experience had demonstrated that university-trained British personnel could handle spoken Russian just as well as native speakers. This broadened the pool of possible recruits. It also got round some of the security risks of employing people with families in Russia or Eastern Europe, which made them vulnerable to Soviet blackmail. It might also be possible to recruit enlisted national servicemen already working elsewhere on monitoring Soviet signals.

Telephone circuits were not the only ones at stake. The Soviet cables also carried telegraphic material. Some of this was encrypted and would have to be sent on to the code-breakers at the NSA in Washington and GCHQ in Cheltenham. But what about the non-encrypted, plaintext, messages? Should the team handling the voice material also handle this? Should the work be done by a separate group? Or should NSA and GCHQ be asked to provide experts of their own to assist?[7]

The men around the table at Carlton Gardens discussed the pros and cons of all these issues before referring them back to Washington. Bill Harvey and Peter Lunn also had to be consulted. Eventually, early in 1954, it was decided to set up two separate processing units, one in Washington and one in London. The Washington unit, run by the CIA and known as the Telegraphic Processing Unit, or TPU, would handle all the telegraphic material and call on the NSA for help with any decryption that was needed, although most of it was not encoded at all. The London unit, handled by SIS, would build on Section Y's experience with the Vienna project to deal with all the telephone material and would be known as the Main Processing Unit, or MPU.

On two vital issues the CIA and SIS agreed. First, they would attack all the circuits that were likely to appear off the three Soviet cables. And, second, there would have to be a small advance processing unit in Berlin itself to handle top priority material. If the main job of the tunnel was to provide advance warning of an attack, then speed would be of the essence. There must be experts on the spot who could instantly recognize crucial indicators of some unexpected Soviet move, avoiding the inevitable delays when the material was sent to Washington or London. Ideally this should be a joint Anglo-American team. No more than ten people would be required: two signals officers, six transcribers, one Russian typist and a secretary. Recruiting should begin in January, training in May, and the team would have to be ready to go to Berlin by August 1954 at the latest. This Berlin unit was known as the Forward Processing Unit, or FPU. As for the other processing units, they would gradually be increased in size, but only as the quality and quantity of the cable intelligence became clear.

The meeting ended amicably on 18 December and Rowlett flew on to Frankfurt to brief Harvey. The CIA Berlin station chief had not been present for the Carlton Gardens meeting; nor for that matter had Lunn. But for another round table meeting at Section Y offices Harvey was present. It took place in March 1955, just as construction on the tunnel was ending and the crucial phone tapping being put into place. Harvey predictably began by emphasizing the vital importance of security, and to make his point he said he hoped no Philbys were present. At this point the Scottish George Young leaped in with a reassuring joke. Yes, he told Harvey, 'we don't want to be caught with our kilts up.'[8]

But it was already too late. Sitting quietly at the table during the December meeting was George Blake, taking copious notes. Afterwards, as instructed by Tom Gimson, he wrote up a record of the three-day meeting. Early in the new year he finished his task and circulated copies to all those involved. But he also kept an extra copy. One evening in mid-January, slipping the yellowy-green carbon paper into his pocket, he left Carlton Gardens, stepped out into the night, and followed his carefully rehearsed routine to meet up with Sergei Kondrashev.

Blake's control had spent the day foiling his British surveillance. First, true to his cover as cultural attaché, he accompanied a departing delegation of Soviet chess players to Heathrow airport. After returning to central London he then spent the day shopping and going to the cinema while a fellow KGB officer checked to see if he was being followed. When the coast was clear he boarded a bus and there, on the top deck, met up with Blake. The SIS officer slipped the Russian the minutes on Stopwatch/Gold, as well as notes on British intercept operations elsewhere. Several stops later Kondrashev got off the bus and was picked up by a car from the Soviet embassy. He immediately reported on the meeting to his KGB superiors. But it took him until mid-February to file a full written report and send on the carbon copy given him by Blake, which was too faded to photocopy. 'The information on a planned intercept operation against internal telephone lines on GDR territory to a radar station is of interest', he noted.[9] This turned out to be one of the most modest understatements of the entire Cold War.

10

Digging Gold

BACK IN WASHINGTON a blissfully unaware Allen Dulles gave his formal approval to the tunnel operation on 20 January 1954, just two days after Blake handed over details to Kondrashev. In Berlin, Harvey took a lease for the land in Rudow and signed a contract with a German builder for the compound. Roughly the site of an average American city block, it was surrounded by high-security chain fencing. Inside was the main operations building with its extra deep basement, a combined barracks and kitchen–dining facility for the staff, and a third building to house the three diesel-driven power generators. On top of the main operations building sat a parabolic antenna. To the outside world this was a radar station.

For the German contractor this was just a routine job for the American occupation forces. By the end of August he had finished work and handed the site over to the Americans. That same day Harvey put in place a super strict security regime. Using 12 × 60 Leitz night infra-red binoculars, twenty-four hour observation of the area between the base and the Schönefelder Chaussee began, with all movements of personnel and vehicles, including the 'Vopos' (the Volkspolizei, or East German police guards), being carefully logged. The log was reviewed periodically for any gradual but significant changes in traffic pattern that might indicate the tunnel had been spotted by the Russians or

Nothing here to suggest the presence of one of the Western allies' most powerful underground weapons against the Red Army. The tunnel began here, at Rudow, from the basement of the left-hand building, disguised as part of a more conventional radar site

East Germans. Idle Vopos spent a lot of time gazing at the warehouse and the other buildings. But nothing suggested any intensified interest or special surveillance.

Harvey was particularly relieved to hear that the residents of Rudow had swallowed the cover story. Hidden microphones were installed on the chain link fence in the hope of picking up Vopo conversations that might reveal what they thought or knew about the site. Before tunnelling began the entire area was swept for microphones or telephone taps. CIA and SIS officers coming in and out travelled in closed three-quarter ton US Army trucks to conceal their presence.

The tunnel itself required special handling. For this Dulles turned to the US Army Corps of Engineers, which was uniquely equipped for the task. Since the American Revolution it had worked on some of America's boldest engineering enterprises, civilian as well as military: building flood control levees along the Mississippi, designing and constructing the Lincoln Memorial, and erecting massive hydro-electric dams on major rivers such as the Tennessee, Missouri and Columbia. In two world wars and again in Korea it constructed air bases and built bridges and railways immediately behind the battle fronts. Steel-lined tunnels were a speciality because they featured in hydro-electric dams. The corps' chief was Lieutenant-General Samuel D. Sturgis Jr, a man who knew Germany well from his previous post as commanding general of the communications zone supporting the United States Army in Europe.

Dulles made the first contact personally. It also helped that Major-General Arthur Trudeau, the head of Army intelligence, was an engineer by training. Knowing the wealth of data the Vienna lines had produced on Soviet forces in Austria and Hungary, he enthusiastically supported the project. By the time the site was ready that summer Sturgis's men had firmed up the engineering plans, selected a crew and even constructed a mock-up tunnel some 150 yards long at the White Sands Missile Proving Ground in New Mexico. SIS was also busy. Its agreement with the CIA spoke of consultation, and a team of Royal Engineers experimented in digging a vertical shaft at Longmoor Camp, the Royal Engineers Railway Transportation Training Centre, in Hampshire, England.[1]

These various experiments confirmed that a tunnel of the projected length would require very special techniques. The Berlin soil was extremely sandy and the risk of collapse was high. So it was decided that the tunnel should be lined for its entire length with steel, making it effectively a long steel tube constructed underground. The danger would be particularly extreme at its face, so for this part of the operation the corps devised a special shield with horizontal 'blinds'. The diggers, working with shovels and picks to hack out the soil, would work under the shield and thus be protected from cave-ins.

The tunnel liner itself was to consist of hundreds of sections of heavy steel plate, each 6 feet in diameter but only 3 inches deep. After the diggers had excavated enough soil, the shield would be forced forward into place using hydraulic jacks, and then a single steel section bolted into place. As the shield was fractionally larger than the steel rings, it meant that there was a gap of about 1½ inches around the liner. To fill this in, screw-type removal plugs were built into every third section of the liner. Then grouting material was forced through under high pressure to fill the gap in order to prevent the earth above from settling and revealing the tunnel from the surface.

Assembling the basic supplies, equipment and personnel took longer than planned, largely because special orders had to be made for the steel liners. Cast in the United States, they were first assembled in a huge army warehouse in Richmond, Virginia, before being shipped out from Norfolk to Bremerhaven for onward transport to Berlin on allied trains travelling through East Germany. This was the first high-risk phase of the entire operation. The East Germans frequently insisted on spot checks of goods travelling through their zone. So all the steel liners were double-crated and banded in heavy wooden containers. They were also subject to severe drop tests before departure to check they were secure. Loaded on to one-and-a-half freight trains, and weighing 125 tons, they arrived safely in the city without any unwelcome East German attention. To maintain the pretence that the site was a radar station, the team of sixteen engineers adopted the uniform of members of the 9539th TSU of the US Army Signal Corps.

Early in September 1954 all was ready. Only one thing remained before digging could begin. This was to determine the exact point, down to the nearest inch, where the horizontal burrowing would have to stop and the engineers should start digging upwards towards the cables. To calculate this, the surveyors needed to place an object of known size as close as possible to the Schönefelder Chaussee. As none existed, they devised the bright idea of throwing a softball over the border. But every time they did, helpful East German border guards threw it back before readings could be taken. In the end, Harvey was forced to decide on another, potentially far more dangerous, trick. He arranged for a US Army vehicle to have a flat tyre at the right spot on the Schönefelder Chaussee. While changing it, one of the men placed a tiny reflector next to the road.

From the warehouse, the surveyors sent a small beam of light that struck the reflector and bounced back. This gave the precise distance between the two points. Knowing this, the engineers were confident they could hit the target within a matter of inches.[2]

That sorted out, the engineers began their work. Their next task was to sink a 20 foot vertical shaft beneath the basement floor of the warehouse. This was relatively easy. But only six days into the excavation potential disaster struck. For a while it cast the entire project into serious doubt.

The feasibility study had predicted that the water table in this part of Berlin was at 32 feet: deep enough not to cause the diggers any problems as the tunnel would be built at a depth of approximately 23 feet. This, with a 6 foot diameter tunnel, would provide a top cover of some 16 feet of earth, enough to smother any construction noise reaching the surface. But after only a few days the engineers suddenly encountered water at 16 feet. Beneath it they discovered a layer of heavy clay 6 feet thick lying above the 'true' water table. A test bore sunk at the other end of the warehouse showed the heavy clay there, too, but at 16½ feet. They had struck what is known as a 'perched' water table. These are hard to predict and frequently fail to show up on geological surveys. Often they are relatively small. Usually test drillings can quickly solve the problem, but it was obviously impossible for the team to conduct drillings outside under the eyes of the border guards.

Alarm bells rang. It seemed to Harvey's team that there were three possible courses of action: they could abandon the project altogether; they could construct the tunnel at a shallower depth; or they could cut through the clay into the sand below and then build the tunnel at a depth that would still be above the real water table. The problem with this idea was twofold. First, nobody could know when the perched clay table ended, and they ran the risk of finding water suddenly and catastrophically cascading into the tunnel from above. And second, if the table extended all the way to the spot where the tap was to take place, they would have to dig vertically up through the clay. Again they would face the problem of water rushing into the excavation.

To abandon the project was inconceivable. First of all, it simply wasn't Harvey's style. 'He wouldn't have allowed a little thing like that to stop him', stressed Montgomery. Besides, the stakes were far too high and the political pressure on the CIA was now intense. In the White House the outwardly placid Eisenhower was clamouring for every shred of intelligence about Soviet intentions and complained bitterly at American failure to deliver it. The Soviet testing of a hydrogen bomb the year before had taken Washington by surprise and deeply dismayed the President. The May Day parade in Moscow just months before unveiled a new heavy Soviet bomber, the Bison, in numbers not predicted by the CIA. 'Our relative position in intelligence', complained the President, 'could scarcely have been worse.'

Even as bulldozers were clearing the tunnel site at Rudow, Eisenhower appointed James Killian, the head of the Massachusetts Institute of Technology, to chair a top secret commission tasked with increasing American capacity 'to get more positive intelligence about the enemy's intentions and capabilities' – otherwise known as the Surprise Attack Panel. Then, in the same month that the tunnel engineers hit the water table, Lieutenant-General James Doolittle submitted a hard-hitting report to the President.

Its background lay in a duel between Dulles and the rabble-rousing anti-communist witch-hunter Senator Joseph McCarthy. After targeting the State Department for hidden communists he now had his eyes on the CIA. Victory had gone to Dulles in the first round, when he refused to allow his officers to appear before Congress and threatened to resign unless McCarthy was called off. But to head off more attacks Eisenhower had agreed to the Doolittle inquiry. Its conclusion was blunt.

The acquisition and proper evaluation of adequate and reliable intelligence on the capabilities and intentions of Soviet

Russia is today's most important military and political requirement . . . We are facing an implacable enemy . . . There are no rules in such a game. Hitherto acceptable norms of human conduct do not apply. If the United States is to survive, long-standing American concepts of 'fair play' must be reconsidered. We must develop effective espionage and counterespionage services and must learn to subvert, sabotage and destroy our enemies by more clever, more sophisticated and more effective methods than those used against us.

Every possible scientific and technical approach to intelligence must be adopted, Doolittle concluded, since the Iron Curtain states made old-fashioned espionage prohibitive in terms of dollars and human lives.

Eisenhower agreed. Soon afterwards the National Security Council issued a directive, NSC 5412, authorizing Dulles and the CIA to proceed as recommended. Dulles knew he could count on Eisenhower's support, but only so long as he delivered.[3] 'The President', writes his biographer, 'intended to fight the Communists just as he had fought the Nazis, on every battle-front, with every available weapon.'[4] One of the most important was the CIA. Its future, and that of Allen Dulles, depended on just such projects as Stopwatch/Gold. Backing down because of an unexpected technical hitch just was not possible.

In London, SIS was coming under similar pressure. Churchill was his usual impatient self in demanding instant information from his Minister of Defence about Soviet strength. And as the tunnel engineers were scratching their heads over the water problem, the Joint Intelligence Committee, sitting in its third floor office in the Ministry of Defence in Whitehall, was debating the likelihood of a 'bolt from the blue', as they called it. Although they eventually dismissed the prospect, British intelligence chiefs stressed how vital early warning intelligence still remained. Miscalculation by one side or another during a period of heightened political tension provided the most likely scenario for war. For that reason, they urged, 'we must be able to watch and analyse military moves and to relate them to the political temperature'.[5]

With Berlin still firmly at the epicentre of the Cold War stand-off, the signal was clear to SIS in general and Lunn in particular. The tunnel must be driven forward at any cost.

★

Harvey and his team explored all the options while British engineers flew in to give their own advice. In early October they decided to go with the second option: to dig the tunnel immediately above the clay level and the perched water table. The tunnel would only be about 9 feet below ground, so they would have to ensure no construction noise reached the surface. They would also install extra water pumps and raise the crucial communications cables well above the tunnel floor. If at any point along the line of construction the clay level fell, they would follow it down. If it rose to the point that construction was becoming too shallow, they would cut through the clay and use heavy pumping equipment to deal with the drainage problems.

The team began digging again on 11 October and the next day manoeuvred the steel shield into place at a depth of 16 feet. After all the pessimism, an ebullient Harvey reported to CIA headquarters in Frankfurt that the horizontal section of the tunnel should be completed by the end of January 1955. He was only a month too optimistic. The job was actually finished on 28 February. By this time the army engineers had been tunnelling for exactly 1,476 feet, roughly the length of the Lincoln Memorial reflecting pool in Washington DC. Over 3,000 tons of soil had been excavated, every pound of which was carefully piled up in the warehouse basement.

As the engineers proceeded, they lined the tunnel with sand-bags to help muffle the noise, increase insulation and provide a shelf for the power and signal cables as well as air-conditioning

Above: *A converted forklift truck in action. Sandbags down the sides of the tunnel helped muffle the noise*

Left: *British and American army engineers digging the tunnel. Ducts from an air-conditioning unit in the warehouse helped keep them cool*

ducts. The bags also had the side benefit of cutting down on the amount of sand that had to be hauled back to the warehouse basement. To help in this tedious task a converted electric fork-lift truck which ran along a wooden track was brought in to pull a string of rubber-tyred trailers backwards and forwards. Wood for the floor and track came from the disassembled containers used to transport the steel rings to Berlin. To the toiling men sweating at the tunnel face, ducts delivered cool air from an air conditioning unit in the warehouse.

Harvey visited the site regularly. But as a known CIA officer he always did so at night, after taking all the usual security measures to ensure he was not followed. One evening he took along Major-General Ben Harrell, the Army's chief of staff in Berlin. 'Harvey and I drove way across Berlin and went into a parking area and changed cars', recalled Harrell. 'It was real cloak and dagger as far as I was concerned. Coming back, Bill asked me to come up and have a drink. He poured me a full glass of scotch without anything else in it. When I finally got home, my wife asked me where I'd been.' Covered with mud and smelling of alcohol, Harrell lamely replied that he'd been out with Bill Harvey on business.[6]

Digging was indeed dirty business. To the outside world the engineers were signals specialists and so they could not afford to be seen in dirty fatigues. Harvey therefore had a washer and dryer installed on site. This proved an extra bonus during one memorably nasty moment. Soon after digging began the engineers uncovered an old cesspit. 'We were almost literally up to our knees in the stuff,' recalled Montgomery, 'it stank and almost gassed the engineers.'[7]

Completion of the tunnel early in 1955 did not mean the job was finished. The tap chamber itself now had to be built. This meant digging vertically upwards into the soft and sandy soil. What would keep everything from collapsing on top of them? Here the British took over. After experimenting out at Gatow airfield, in the British sector of the city, John Wyke had come up with an ingenious device consisting of a large cylinder with a

Down the rough wooden track in the centre of the tunnel ran a converted electric forklift truck on rubber tyres that removed the soil and brought in heavy equipment

Only two feet below the surface of the Schönefelder Chausee, the tap chamber is being dug; horizontal removable slats hold back the sandy soil which hampered the excavation

series of slots at the top. The cylinder was placed vertically in the tunnel and the soil then removed slot by slot before the whole device was levered upwards.

It worked. The engineers began digging upwards on 10 March and finished eighteen days later with the three target cables completely exposed. By now they were only inches below the surface. Whenever an East German patrol passed overhead, they stopped work. Yet another problem now threatened the project. A build-up of moisture endangered the sophisticated electronic tapping equipment that had to be installed. To guard against it, the engineers insulated the section of the tunnel immediately adjacent to the tap chamber with marine-type plywood to form a closed room and erected vapour barriers. In addition, they erected a heavy anti-personnel door of steel and concrete to seal off the tunnel some 15 yards from its terminal end.[8]

Now the final and most sensitive part of the operation had to be installed: the tap itself. This was a physical tap, which meant first exposing the Soviet cables by stripping them of their covering and then attaching wires to draw off the signals. SIS's moment had finally arrived. John Wyke, drawing on the experience and skill he had acquired in Vienna, triumphantly brought it off without a hitch.

Tapping a line is a task that always teeters on the edge of disaster. It involves drawing off some degree of power from the target cable, but this can easily alert the cable users to the fact that something is wrong. The trick is to carry out what experts call a 'high-impedance' tap. This means drawing off as small and as unnoticeable a signal as possible, and it requires a skilled and steady hand. Difficult at the best of times, it would be an almost impossible task in the dark and cramped conditions of the tunnel, where noise had to be kept to an absolute minimum. To add to the discomfort, the tap chamber had to be pressurized while Wyke toiled at his job. This was necessary because the Soviet cables might have been pressurized, a precaution sometimes taken to provide an additional warning of a tap. A cut into the covering of the wires would instantly cause the pressure to drop and raise the alarm. The Soviet cables were not, in fact, pressurized, but Wyke had to assume they were.

Another tricky problem now emerged for the engineers. The high-impedance tap itself also imposed a challenge. To be comprehensible to those listening in, the signal had to be amplified. Yet the longer the distance between the point of the tap and the amplifier – in other words, the further the signal had to pass – the more noise or interference it picked up along the cable. As the signal was weak to begin with, it meant that the pre-amplification chamber had to be built as close as possible to the tap chamber. Here the signals were isolated before being amplified and sent on to the warehouse for recording. 'The lead-away cables', notes the CIA history, 'were constructed of the best available materials, sheathed in lead, and handled in accordance with the highest company standards.' All the heavy electronic equipment had to be transported along the length of the tunnel and the pre-amplification chamber constructed literally under the boots of the Vopos above. Once installed and running, it also further raised the temperature inside the tunnel.

Completion of the tap came none too soon. On the same day the engineers began work on the tap chamber, the Joint Intelligence Committee met again in London. Both Sir John Sinclair, the SIS chief, and Sir Dick White, the head of MI5, were present to hear Brigadier Way of the Joint Intelligence Board highlight the discrepancy between American and British intelligence estimates on the amount of military equipment passing from Russia to East Germany. Some discrepancy was inevitable, he admitted, given that the Americans had better cover and more sources than SIS. But it was desirable they work hard to get agreement. Still, and once again, the allies were slightly out of step. Stopwatch/Gold held the promise of settling their differences.[9]

★

'We knew from the very beginning that the tunnel had a finite life', confessed Allen Dulles much later. While construction inched forward, Harvey and Lunn had worked together on hammering

The Forward Operations Chamber with its pre-amplifiers. The Russians were flabbergasted at the sight when they descended the tunnel

out an agreement both on what more should be done to protect the tunnel from discovery and on how to respond if the Soviets discovered it. One way or another, Harvey argued, they certainly would. But like everyone else, he had no idea that they already had. In November he flew out to Washington for a meeting with Dulles to go over the project almost literally inch by inch. As a result they decided to put several extra security measures in place.

One was to install on the near side of the pre-amp chamber (the side closest to the Western entrance to the tunnel) a heavy torch-proof steel door set in substantial concrete slabs with a lock and bar that would be wired with an alarm system to prevent tampering. The door would be kept locked at all times except when individuals were actually in the chamber itself, and a telephone system would be installed to connect the area with the rest of the tunnel. Once the door was in place, Harvey audaciously had the following inscription written on the tap chamber

side in both German and Cyrillic: ENTRY IS FORBIDDEN
BY ORDER OF THE COMMANDING GENERAL. It was
a warning that he thought might give pause to hierarchy-
conscious Soviet and East German officials and gain time for his
team to evacuate the tunnel.

He and Dulles also agreed that steel doors would seal off the
tunnel at the near end, where it crossed the building line of the
warehouse, as well as on the ramp that led from the ground floor
of the warehouse down to the basement and construction area.
At the point where the tunnel actually crossed from the
American into the Soviet sector (about 100 yards from the warehouse), a 40 foot length would be mined using C-3 plastic explosive inserted into a sealed garden hose threaded behind the liner
plate. The hose would contain enough explosive to collapse the
tunnel without causing a major surface eruption. But the explosive would be laid only at the last minute, when an emergency
was imminent.

What if an emergency did occur – if, for example, the
watchers above ground detected Soviet or East German activity that suggested they were poised to discover the tunnel? The
plan hatched out in Washington laid down that all personnel
working in the tunnel itself would be immediately evacuated
back to the Rudow end and the steel doors shut behind them.
Meanwhile Harvey would be notified at his CIA office in
Clayallee, by two-way radio if for any reason the telephone
system was down. Depending on the time available, as much
of the equipment as possible in the tunnel would be removed.
But if discovery was imminent and it seemed likely that Soviet
or East German troops would venture along the tunnel, then
the mined area would be blown. Both Dulles and Harvey
agreed that the commanding officer at the site should have
orders to resist unwanted entry into the tunnel 'with all means
at his disposal'.

And if the worst happened and Moscow discovered the
tunnel? Dulles decided, after considerable discussion, not to brief
the American ambassador in Germany, James Conant, on the

operation. Genuine ignorance of Stopwatch/Gold would give his inevitable public reaction to its discovery a fully authentic flavour. Dulles firmly laid down the line to be followed. The official American reaction was to be 'flat, indignant denial ascribing any such protest to a baseless enemy provocation'.[10]

11

Turning On the Tap

EARLY IN 1955, as the engineers approached the end of their task, George Blake arrived to take up a new position with SIS in Berlin. With Stopwatch/Gold now under way, his position as deputy to Tom Gimson at Section Y in Carlton Gardens had been taken by an officer from the CIA. By now Blake was married, and he and his wife settled into a top floor flat on Platanenallee in Charlottenburg, a smart residential part of the city that had escaped the worst of allied bombing, about ten minutes walk away from the SIS compound.

Lunn was firmly in place as the station's dynamic head, his team very different from the one he had captained during the 1936 Olympics. It was well financed, with its bills paid out of the occupation costs, which in turn were absorbed by the German taxpayer; and it operated at the cutting edge of British Cold War intelligence. In such conditions Lunn was in his element. Some of those working for him thought he appeared 'a bit of a go-getter', impatient of detail. But they admired and respected his vision and energy.

A decade into the Cold War Berlin remained the epicentre of international espionage and offered the best opportunity for establishing direct contact with Soviet personnel. The sector boundary between the Eastern and Western halves of the city was not yet sealed off: the wall still lay six years in the future.

Checkpoints existed on all the main streets crossing the border but none on minor crossings or on the U-Bahn, the city's still unified underground system, and people could cross freely in both directions. Blake, with his appreciation of big city transport finely honed through his frequent clandestine meetings with Kondrashev in London, marvelled that 'it was as easy to travel from West to East Berlin and back as from Hammersmith to Piccadilly'.[1]

Blake had nothing officially to do with Stopwatch/Gold while he was in Berlin, where only Lunn, his station deputy, Jimmy Munn, and John Wyke were briefed on it. What Blake knew derived exclusively from his former position in Section Y, plus anything passed on to him by his KGB control, with whom he immediately made contact. Instead, ironically, as a member of the station's section attempting to penetrate Soviet headquarters in Karlshorst, he found himself cultivating members of the KGB and attempting to recruit them as double agents. Here he continued his trade in treachery, handing over to the KGB as much material as he could about SIS (and CIA) operations.

In one sense Blake's position was now easier because his contacts with known KGB officers could be explained away by his official duties. On the other it was much more precarious. Unlike during his time at Section Y, he now shared an office at the Olympic Stadium with a colleague, and photographing documents proved risky: he was more afraid than ever of being unexpectedly interrupted while at work with his Minox camera. 'Nevertheless,' he recalled, 'as I was always on the look out for an opportunity to photograph, I usually found one, though sometimes, in cases of great ugency, I had to take a deliberate risk and just hope for the best.'

Despite the risks, Blake carefully disguised any tension he felt. Lunn considered him the best agent runner he had. In the summer of 1955 an old wartime SIS officer and Unionist Member of Parliament from Northern Ireland, Harford Montgomery Hyde, visited Berlin and made a courtesy call on Lunn. Blake came into the room and Lunn introduced him. After he had left, Lunn remarked to the MP 'what a good agent' Blake was turning out to be.[2] Soon afterwards Wyke completed the tap on the Soviet cables beneath the Schönefelder Chaussee. Stopwatch/Gold, one of the most audacious Cold War operations ever launched jointly by SIS and CIA, was finally under way.

★

Yet even as it began, critics might have wondered if it were already obsolete. The icy political climate appeared to be finally melting after Stalin's death. It was not just that a carefree peace-time mood has taken hold in the West, with Disneyland opening its doors in California, Davy Crockett coonskin hats all the rage, Bill Haley's *Rock around the Clock* sweeping the hit parade and Vladimir Nabokov's novel *Lolita* causing outrage on both sides of the Atlantic. More serious milestones were being established. The same month the tunnel taps began the Federal Republic of Germany at last regained its sovereignty and was admitted to Nato. Occupation troops of all four wartime allies finally quit Austria, as well as their various tunnel operations there. Simultaneously Moscow created the Warsaw Pact, with the German Democratic Republic as a full and founding member. This appeared to cement the division of Europe, signal Soviet acceptance of the status quo, and lift the threat of Red Army incursion into the West.

But as the ice cracked it released powerful and unpredictable currents. Nikita Khrushchev, the emerging new Soviet leader, was volatile and unpredictable. In July he offered a powerful reminder to Western spy chiefs of why Stopwatch/Gold was still needed. The occasion was the long-awaited Geneva Summit Conference at the United Nations' Palais des Nations, attended by leaders of all the four great powers: Eisenhower, Eden, Edgar Faure of France, and Khrushchev and Bulganin for the Soviet Union.

Ten years after Hitler's death the conference was intended to relax Cold War tensions and set a benchmark for peace.

Unexpectedly, Eisenhower unveiled a dramatic proposal suggesting that the United States and the Soviet Union exchange a complete blueprint of their military establishments and open their skies to allow reconnaissance planes to take all the pictures they wanted. Both superpowers, he admitted frankly, possessed new and terrible weapons and his plan – immediately nicknamed 'Open Skies' – would, he suggested, significantly reduce the possibility of surprise attack and thus reduce tensions. Khrushchev quickly and bluntly denounced the idea as 'a bald espionage plot' and the proposal died on the table.[3]

With it faded easy hopes of relaxation in world tension, and soon the volume of threatening rhetoric was escalating ominously again. In Moscow, Khrushchev famously promised to bury the West, while John Foster Dulles chillingly laid out his philosophy of brinkmanship. 'The ability to get on the verge without getting into war is the necessary art', he declared. 'If you are scared to go to the brink, you are lost.' J. Robert Oppenheimer, the distinguished American nuclear scientist, compared the United States and Russia to two scorpions in a bottle. The atomic clock, he warned, was ticking 'faster and faster'.

★

If the skies were closed then the reconnaissance underground would have to begin. Wyke and his team inserted the first successful tap of Stopwatch/Gold on 11 May 1955, switching on a vast stream of intelligence that over the next eleven months was to be fed into Western intelligence reports, identified only as 'a clandestine source of established authenticity'. The bare statistics alone are impressive. The three cables being tapped carried some 1,200 communications channels, with the maximum number of channels being used at any one time amounting to 500. On average, 28 telegraphic and 121 telephone circuits were continuously recorded on Ampex tape recorders, using about 50,000 reels of magnetic tape. In all, they eventually weighed some 25 tons.

*John Foster Dulles,
apostle of Cold War
brinkmanship and
American Secretary of
State during
Stopwatch/Gold. His
brother Allen headed
the CIA*

*The overground complex at Rudow which provided cover for the tunnel,
whose route is marked by the dotted line leading to Alt-Glienicke and the
Schönefelder Chaussee in the distance. This photograph was taken in 1964,
after construction of the Berlin Wall, which can be clearly seen with its
accompanying watch-towers*

Hidden in the warehouse basement at Rudow, rows of amplifiers and voltage stabilizers maintain a steady flow of messages from the cable taps to the transcribers and translators

Such a quantity of raw material required enormous investments of space and personnel to process and analyse it into a usable form for consumers. In London alone, at the Main Processing Unit, SIS employed at its peak over 300 people, who transcribed and translated some 20,000 Soviet two-hour voice reels containing some 368,000 conversations. In addition, they received 13,500 German two-hour voice reels, processing some 5,500 of them, containing 75,000 conversations, of which 17,000 were fully transcribed.

Work on the teletype traffic was carried out in Washington. Here, in a CIA unit housed in one of the buildings run by the agency's clandestine services division known as T-32, a team of 350 people fluent in Russian or German toiled, fifty at a shift, in a windowless room known as the 'Hosiery Mill'. Situated in a prefabricated building along the Washington Mall, it got its name from the ribbons of communications wire that festooned its interior. The floor sagged under the weight of the machinery and the building was clad in steel to prevent the escape of elec-tronic emissions that might just be picked up by the Russians. 'It is greatly in your interest to know', announced the deputy chief of the section, 'where any of this material is coming from. For the opposition to stop the flow all they would need to know is that we have this many Russian and German speakers together.'[4]

The Washington team completely transcribed 18,000 six-hour teletype Soviet reels and 11,000 six-hour German teletype reels. Many of these contained as many as 18 separate circuits, so that the potential of any single six-hour reel was approximately 216 hours of teletype messages. Some were in plaintext, others in cipher, and these were passed on to the National Security Agency for treatment. The daily output measured about 4,000 feet and printed in book form would have filled a space 10 feet wide, 15 feet long and 8 feet high.

In Berlin itself, housed at the Rudow site, a small advance pro-cessing unit of two to four linguists carried out on-the-spot monitoring of the cables for any signs of detection as well as scanning the more productive circuits for 'hot' intelligence. The machine for monitoring the relevant circuits was known as 'the egg-beater'. Immediate and important items were sent electron-ically to Washington and London.

But the bulk of the intercepts, the voice and teletype reels, were first packaged up in carefully camouflaged boxes, taken from the Rudow site in an army truck and then flown by special military flights to the United States and Britain.[5] Tight security rules remained in place and the fiction firmly maintained that Rudow was a purely army base with no connection at all with the CIA.

By this time Hugh Montgomery was acting as the principal link between Harvey at the CIA base in Dahlem and Vyrl Lichleiter at Rudow. 'I'd meet up with Vyrl in my car some-where on the outskirts of the city late at night', he recalled. 'We'd unload the contents of the truck into the trunk of my car and I'd then take it back to the base after handing over to Vyrl some boxes of new and unused tapes.' After a while they ran out of different places to meet and fell to regularly exchanging boxes in the Grünewald.

In the CIA Berlin office the registry chief bitterly complained about their weight. Not being in on Stopwatch/Gold, he was told simply that the packages contained processed uranium ore smuggled out by agents from the uranium–mining operation set up in the Erzgebirge mountains by a corporation known as Wismut. After that, he shut up.[6] All in all, by the time circulation of the Stopwatch/Gold halted in 1958, 90,000 translated messages or telephone conversations had been circulated, resulting in 1,750 separate intelligence reports.

12

Chester Terrace

To house the small army of transcribers and analysts SIS took possession of several addresses on Chester Terrace, an exclusive street of porticoed Regency houses designed by John Nash on the edge of Regent's Park. Adjacent was the Chester Gate home of John Profumo, who was soon to be engulfed in one of the greatest sex scandals of British history, and his glamorous wife, the former film star Valerie Hobson. Just a stone's throw away was the White House, a fashionable apartment block on Albany Street housing a high-living businessman and seller of vending machines known as Gordon Lonsdale. In reality he was Konon Molody, one of the most gifted KGB moles ever to operate in London. From here he ran the infamous Portland spy ring until his arrest some five years later.

Heading the on-site Chester Terrace team were Brigadier Eric Greer, who had been British military attaché in Moscow during the Second World War, an RAF squadron leader named Brinley Ryan and a CIA officer known only as 'Fred'.[1] Overseeing the entire operation was the now veteran tunnel expert Andrew King, who divided his time between SIS headquarters in Broadway and a subsidiary office in Chester Gate. The car-crazy King had long ago discarded the chauffeur-driven Jaguar of his glory days in Vienna. Now he buzzed around London in a BMW 'bubble car' that looked like a gigantic raindrop.

Behind the dignified Regency façade of these houses on Chester Terrace was hidden one of the greatest secrets of the Cold War – the army of SIS and CIA workers extracting the latest intelligence from the Berlin Tunnel

The whole operation was given top security. Entry to the buildings was controlled by unarmed guards, and special alarms provided night-time protection. Only the chief CIA officer, 'Fred', was allowed to go anywhere near the CIA offices in London, and then after taking extreme measures to conceal the true nature of the operation. This embarrassingly backfired when British civil servants working in nearby offices of the Ministry of Agriculture reported that American spies were gaining entry to adjacent buildings; they were quietly assured that all was in order.

Working under military cover, CIA officer Joe Evans arrived in London in December 1954 with a couple of other Americans to organize procedures dealing with the tunnel material. His own main task was to analyse the GRU conversations. A graduate of Bucknell University, he had joined the CIA after working as a journalist in his home state of Pennsylvania. He was assigned to Staff D working with Frank Rowlett and before long was analysing bi-weekly SIS reports from the Vienna operation. Rumour had it that these were flown into Washington by the British state-owned BOAC airline under the pilot's seat. One of his earliest small triumphs involved the Red Army's Central Group of Forces. 'We got the volume of flour consumed within a specific period. We also got the rations of the Red Army. From that I helped extrapolate the manpower of the Central Group. Later information confirmed I was right', he remembered.

Evans found SIS frantically recruiting transcribers and linguists. Some of them shifted over from Section Y's work on the Vienna tunnels but this was not enough. So SIS began to trawl through the army and air force lists for retired officers who could speak Russian, handle intelligence material or otherwise lend a hand. They recruited retired Indian Army colonels and even veterans from the Boer War. British code-breakers at GCHQ also played a part by providing some of their own trained analysts and linguists to help out. 'There was such a flood of material that everyone was called in to help', recalled one GCHQ veteran. The situation looked ripe for the outbreak of a turf war between

SIS and the code-breakers over ownership of the material. In fact the urgency and volume of material overwhelmed such instincts.

There were lots of *émigré* Poles. One of the most memorable was a cavalry officer with a sabre cut and eyepatch. 'All the women swooned', said Evans. 'He was extremely gallant and there were some pretty good parties.' Another had been a minister in the pre-war Polish government and was almost deaf. Then there was the chief linguist, a Russian named Mike, who was rumoured to be the last graduate of the Tsarist naval academy and who had badly injured a leg parachuting into Yugoslavia during the war. He married one of his subordinates, a White Russian named Nina from Harbin who sported a boa and brandished a cigarette holder. 'She was the widow of a British officer killed in Korea', recalled Evans, 'a real spark plug at parties. A lot of us were invited to the wedding down in Catford. It was pretty boisterous and ended up in a fistfight.'

For many of the Polish *émigrés*, stranded in Britain by the communist takeover of their homeland, the pittance they were paid for the hours of tedious transcription threw them a vital financial lifeline. Evans remembered that few of the women had much more than a single change of dress. They toiled exceptionally hard for little material reward and he admired their commitment and diligence. 'They were paid peanuts', he recalled. The eventual closure of the unit in 1958 caused a lot of them severe hardship. Although there still remained about half a million hours of unprocessed conversations on the tapes, by then the Stopwatch/Gold material was outdated and useless. The Polish ex-minister, remembered Evans, ended up as a dishwasher in a London hotel.

Rubbing shoulders with this exotic mix were a handful of British linguists who had studied Russian in Britain. Some of them had been sent by SIS to live with Russian *émigrés* in Paris to perfect the language. But others arrived fresh out of school. This caused a problem. Red Army telephone conversations were not just idiomatic but liberally peppered with obscenities that not everyone understood. To spare blushes all round it was decided to produce a glossary of terms, which could be privately consulted. 'Two copies arrived from Washington', remembered Evans, 'labelled TOP SECRET OBSCENE.'

The Anglo-American team shared beers round the corner in the Chester Arms, where they earnestly debated the merits of war movies such as *Ice Cold in Alex* and *Bridge on the River Kwai*. Occasionally there were staff parties. A huge ground-floor room was cleared, drinks flowed freely and the cosmopolitan army of listeners-in let down their hair and discharged their pent-up energies dancing to the strains of favourites such as Glen Miller's 'Kalamazoo' and 'Chattanooga Choo-choo' or jiving to the shocking new beat of rock 'n' roll. It was also the year of Rex Harrison and *My Fair Lady*; before the show even opened in the West End the Americans were able to snap up the record in the local US Army stores.

Only one event cast any shadow across these sunny uplands of inter-allied harmony: the Suez crisis of 1956. Britain's attack on Egypt split the Chester Terrace team along national lines. 'The one really bad spot', remembered Evans, 'was when the Royal Navy was ordered to interdict American ships trying to get close to the action. Unfortunately this also coincided with the Hungarian uprising. Tempers got pretty hot and I was pretty annoyed myself and debates took up so much time that an official notice came round telling us to desist.' But none of this stopped the joint work. It was by no means the only occasion when a political storm between London and Washington barely rippled the surface of transatlantic intelligence co-operation. Even then, however, each partner shared only what it needed to. Alongside the CIA team worked an SIS counter-intelligence expert. While carefully poring over the tunnel material, he kept his opinions to himself and never gave the Americans any feedback of his own.

Otherwise the work was dismayingly routine. The small army of transcribers, listening to the tapes on Ampex tape recorders, wrote down in Russian what they heard. They had to stop and restart the tape to catch single words. Sometimes they came to

The main offices of the Chester Terrace operation overlooking Regent's Park. Here the cosmopolitan army of eavesdroppers would occasionally let their hair down to the rhythms of Glenn Miller

recognize individual speakers by their voices. At other times they would simply note inconsequential sequences of talk without actually writing them down, concentrating instead on the high-lights. They would then show these to someone higher up the chain of command for a decision about whether a full or summary translation was needed. Eventually the GRU material landed on Joe Evans's desk for detailed analysis.

About the top priority Evans remains emphatic. 'The grim-mest scenario was of a surprise attack, a "cold start" without the call-up of reserves or the transfer of units to a forward area', he recorded.

> The likeliest attackers would be the seven armies of the Group of Soviet Forces Germany . . . readying [them] to strike would, of course, necessitate communication on the GSFG landlines monitored by CIA and MI6 . . . The surest indicators were expected to emerge from chatter about the transfer of landline service from stationery GSFG barracks throughout East Germany to temporary locations closer to the West German border, closer to Nato forces . . . Early warning . . . was the most compelling justification for the operation.[2]

Evans's 'cold start' was what British intelligence chiefs described as the 'bolt from the blue'. It explained why the Stopwatch/Gold leaders had insisted on the need for a Forward Processing Unit at the tunnel site itself. It was here that the first warning of a possible attack would come as the Red Army began shuffling its telephone lines for the use of its forward units. Even before he left Washington, Evans had this drilled into him by an episode that occurred shortly after he began working with Rowlett's team:

> For the huge commitment of dollars early warning was the *vital item*. I know this. A call came down from on high from some Deputy Director in the CIA asking the reason for the

commitment. Would someone please explain he demanded. I was the only one around. I was really nervous. I took a map of East Germany and laid out where the military units were placed and why we needed the operation. That did the job.

★

Doing his job on the front line itself, in Berlin, was another CIA officer named David Murphy. Eventually head of the CIA's Soviet bloc division, he had trained and dispatched agents into Russia from Bavaria in the 1940s and was fluent in both German and Russian. In the summer of 1954 he was chosen as deputy to Bill Harvey, whom he succeeded. The tempestuous Berlin station chief had already discarded other candidates. So the hardened and experienced Murphy decided to take a special approach.

'I met Bill for lunch in the summer of '54 in Washington. I knew that he didn't really want a deputy and had already chewed out some other candidates', he recalled, 'so I suggested that my special job should be to review all the material we were getting in about the KGB base in Karlshorst – in other words be his chief of Soviet operations and run the "target room" in our Berlin base. So that's what I did while the tunnel was in operation.'[3]

Murphy was briefed about the tunnel by Harvey only after he had arrived in the city. 'I arrived and there were no flags flying and no music so I got myself organised and found a house and didn't even know the tunnel was being dug. But when the taps were about to appear Bill said " you need to know about this".' The instant they began to come through Murphy realized their worth. Comparing them with other material collected by the target room he knew they were authentic. One of the comparative sources was Brixmis, along with its American counterpart, the US military liaison mission. Another was the high-level Soviet defector Lieutenant-Colonel Pyotr Popov. Since being recruited by the CIA in Vienna, Popov had been transferred by

Moscow to Schwerin in East Germany and was Harvey's most important inside source on Soviet military intelligence. 'We could look at his stuff, mostly about GRU Schwerin operations into the West, and compare it with the other stuff we had', Murphy recalled.

There was only one problem. Because of the tight security surrounding the tunnel virtually no one else in the target room knew of it. So Murphy could not disclose the source and had to keep everything on a completely separate card file. 'This was a bitch', he recalled, 'but I'd bring it to Harvey and he loved it. This is where we really got to know each other.' [4] Murphy, no mean operator himself, regarded Harvey as the best he had ever met. 'Bill was as smart as a whip', he remembered.

Their camaraderie was at its most intense working within arm's length of the enemy down at the tunnel itself. Here, sitting side by side with the army of technicians listening in to the Russians talking between Karlshorst, Zossen-Wünsdorf and Moscow, the two men strained to detect any clues of impending attack. When not doing that, they basked in the plentiful harvest of material that was manna for the counter-intelligence experts.

The British also had their men at the site doing the same. For security reasons Lunn usually stayed well away, just as he did from the CIA base on Clayallee. Instead he left the work to John Wyke. Here, as in London, the allies worked as a team, scanning the Cold War front line for any hint of danger.

13

'A Bonanza'

As OPPORTUNITIES AROSE, the tunnel's targets rapidly expanded to include an astonishing range of political, military and operational intelligence. Despite Stalin's death, the West was still largely in the dark about conditions in the Soviet Union and its satellites. Berlin itself was the focus of some of the richest data. A major source of British and American anxiety was that Moscow would hand over control of the city to the East Germans. The German Democratic Republic was fully recognized by Moscow and there was a Soviet embassy on the Unter den Linden. Moscow agreed that the German Democratic Republic could, at last, have its own official army. Until then it had masqueraded simply as a paramilitary police force. News of this decision first reached the West by means of tunnel intelligence in time for a foreign ministers' meeting in Geneva in October 1955.

But the Ulbricht regime wanted more: Soviet recognition of the GDR's claim to full sovereignty over the city. This opened up a nightmare scenario for the West. If Moscow gave up its occupying rights in the city, would this affect the rights of the Western powers? Would the GDR dictator move to starve or seize West Berlin by closing off access routes in a replay of Stalin's earlier blockade? Public pronouncements by Khrushchev and other Soviet leaders were not reassuring.

Fortunately Stopwatch/Gold told another story. It revealed

that Moscow did not intend to abandon its occupying rights and hand over control to the East Germans. Relations with its German satellite were far from harmonious on this precarious issue. The tunnel provided a vivid picture of the confusion and indecision among Soviet and East German officials whenever an incident occurred in East Berlin involving citizens of the Western powers. Who should deal with them? The East Germans or the Soviets? The inability of the two communist allies to agree provided a signal that Moscow was not yet ready to hand over full control of Berlin to Ulbricht, intelligence that was immensely reassuring. Only in November 1958, long after Stopwatch/Gold had ended, did Khrushchev make a sudden about-turn by demanding that the Western powers renounce their rights in the city. That was the opening shot of the crisis that reached a climax with the building of the wall in August 1961.

Stopwatch/Gold also provided key intelligence on the fall-out from Khrushchev's denunciation of Stalin at the 20th Soviet Party Congress in February 1956. In calling for reforms and a new collective leadership for the Soviet Union he released forces inside the Soviet Union and the satellite states that he found it hard to control. The most dramatic impact was felt in Hungary, where later that year a popular mass uprising briefly threw off the Soviet shackles. The thrust of the speech was too rich and extraordinary for the delegates to keep to themselves. One of the triumphs of Stopwatch/Gold came in capturing a telephone conversation between the wife of Marshal Andrei Grechko, the Soviet commander in East Germany, who had flown to Moscow for the Congress with his wife, and their adult daughter back in Berlin.

In London, Joe Evans patched together evidence of the dramatic fall-out from Khruschev's shocking denunciation of Stalin, which he remembered as easily the most important and exciting piece of intelligence ever processed in Chester Terrace.

It was all in bits and pieces and wasn't extracted from a single 'piece of intelligence'. Rather the story emerged as we translated and collated relevant items from a substantial number of conversations – all credit to the linguists and analysts. At one end were influential Soviets in East Germany, at the other their relatives and friends who either attended or gossiped with those who did. Although the speech was ostensibly secret hundreds attended the congress and a lot of them instantly got on the phone back to Zossen-Wünsdorf . . . so that's how we got it. I remember that Grechko's wife was with him and their daughter remained behind. Madame Grechko spoke daily to her over the tapped phone. She was always complaining about not being able to get her rose garden properly pruned. Once she got on the phone and told her daughter: 'Daddy was invited to dinner by Voroshilov'. 'What did he do?' asked the daughter. 'He shat in his pants', replied Madame Grechko.[1]

As Evans slowly assembled the puzzle and sent it on to Washington, someone had the bright idea of speeding up the process by sending a regular 'highlight' cable containing the most important items. 'I well remember the headline I wrote', he recalled. Given the worship of Stalin, it was astonishing: 'Khrushchev denigrates Stalin.' The new Soviet leader had done the unthinkable and in front of the communist vanguard had taken a sledgehammer to their icon. Eventually the story dribbled through the Iron Curtain and the Americans obtained and released the full text. But for a brief while Stopwatch/Gold had been sitting on a scoop. Major changes were clearly in store. What they meant in practice was unclear, and Stopwatch/Gold would have to help decipher the puzzle.

The ripples were quickly felt in the Soviet Union. One impact was on its nuclear programme. Nuclear scientists had long chafed under tight political control and they seized on Khrushchev's denunciation to win more intellectual and professional freedom. This led to a backlash by hardliners, who desperately attempted to rein in the scientists. Tunnel material provided a detailed account of the crisis and helped identify several hundred personalities involved with the Soviet atomic energy programme.

On the face of it, Berlin and Stopwatch/Gold may seem to have opened a curious window from which to gaze on the Soviet nuclear programme. But East Germany was the most important source of uranium for Stalin's atomic bomb project, and the Soviet dictator had ruthlessly exploited these German resources. Combined with his general policy of using German industry as well as captured German scientists to help rebuild and develop the post-war Soviet Union, this meant that Germany provided one of the most important sources for American and British intelligence on the Soviet nuclear build-up.

The Wismut mining operations quickly became a key target for SIS and the CIA. As early as 1948 General Lucius D. Clay, the American commander in Berlin, had reported that a Soviet corporation known as Wismut had been formed to mine uranium ore (using forced labour) from the rich deposits found in the Erzgebirge mountains near Zwickau in south-west Saxony, along the border with Czechoslovakia. Nominally a joint venture with the East Germans, in reality it was controlled by Moscow. Every ounce of its uranium was shipped to the Soviet Union.[2] SIS and CIA also targeted other East German sites involved with the Soviet bomb production. One was a former IG Farben plant at Bitterfeld, and another was the Tewa plant at Neustadt, both of them now turned into Soviet joint stock companies administered by the directorate of Soviet property in Germany. By recruiting agents in the directorate as well as the companies involved, SIS and CIA made some crucial breakthroughs. The most important was that the Soviets were aiming for a plutonium bomb and that progress was far more advanced than hitherto expected. The interrogation of returning prisoners of war from the Soviet Union and the defection of a key Soviet official at Wismut further enriched the picture. So did the interception of radio signals carrying information about shipments of material from East Germany to the Soviet atomic facility at Yelektrostal, near Moscow, where Uranium-235 was under production. All this gave Berlin a vital part in tracking the Soviet bomb.[3]

But Stopwatch/Gold added even more. It pinpointed certain locations inside the Soviet Union hitherto unsuspected of being connected with atomic research and development and added greatly to knowledge about the workings of Wismut. This was not surprising. The KGB unit with Wismut reported directly to headquarters in Karlshorst on one of the lines being tapped. It had a further value, too, as David Murphy later noted. 'This information could not have come at a better time. Hundreds of German scientists who had participated in the Soviet atomic program and related weapons development were being released.' Among them was a key group of atomic scientists known as the '1037 (P) group' – so-called from their postal address in the Soviet Union. British and American intelligence immediately targeted them for possible defection. Many were tempted by lucrative offers of work and housing, and those who co-operated were interrogated by SIS or CIA over the summer of 1955. Intelligence services need sources to cross-check information. With its stream of hard intelligence on the Soviet nuclear programme, Stopwatch/Gold, wrote Murphy, 'provided a way to crosscheck their statements during debriefing'.[4]

Another fall-out from Khrushchev's destruction of Stalin's reputation was the effort by Marshal Zhukov to curtail the influence of the political commissars in the Red Army. Zhukov had been the outstanding Red Army leader of the Second World War and commander of the forces that stormed Berlin in 1945. Pushed aside by Stalin, who feared his power, he re-emerged under Khrushchev as Minister of Defence. The war hero immediately began a major restructuring and modernization of Soviet forces that involved a powerful assault on political influence in the Red Army. Along with a devastating attack on Stalin's war leadership, these efforts by Zhukov alienated Politburo hardliners, who fought back bitterly. Significant traces of this battle were picked up by Stopwatch/Gold. So was intelligence about a major reorganization of the Soviet Ministry of Defence, the internal organization of the Warsaw Pact, the Eastern bloc riposte to West Germany's admission into NATO and the implementation of

Khrushchev's public promise to reduce the size of the Soviet armed forces. It also helped identify by name several thousand officers in the Red Army and fixed details of Soviet ground forces in the Soviet Union. All this, David Murphy remembered, proved 'a goldmine for order-of-battle analysts'.[5]

One significant effect of the Khrushchev–Zhukov reforms was to strengthen the Soviets' nuclear capabilities. This, too, was tracked by the Stopwatch/Gold analysts, who soon began noting improvements in the nuclear delivery capability in the Soviet Air Force in East Germany, its re-equipment with new bombers and twin-jet interceptors with airborne radar capability, the doubling of its bomber strength in Poland, the location of about 100 previously unknown Soviet air force installations and details about Soviet training plans for early 1956 in Poland and East Germany. They also recorded a reduction in the status and personnel of Soviet naval forces and details of the organization and administrative procedures of the Soviet Baltic Fleet and Soviet naval bases along the Baltic coast.

In London, Joe Evans recorded other intelligence nuggets. Stopwatch/Gold revealed that the Red Army's new T-52 tanks based in East Germany were prone to disabling equipment failures and that 'poor public education and military training, low morale, and barely acceptable discipline' prevailed among low-ranking Soviet conscripts. Soviet officers were reluctant to take initiatives and constantly referred to Moscow for the most elementary decisions. Rampant duplicity and lying infected both the Red Army in Germany and the defence ministry in Moscow. By extrapolation, noted Evans, this provided 'a broad view of the Soviet military and one more major plus for the tunnel'.[6] One small but significant coup achieved by the Chester Terrace team was to solve the code used in radio communications to identify blocks of air space protected by the Soviet Air Defence Command. Not even NSA or GCHQ had managed to decipher it; the RAF officers at Regent's Park did it by careful plaintext analysis.

Among the hardest-hit targets of Stopwatch/Gold were

Soviet military intelligence and counter-intelligence units in East Germany. 'Because these services represented the single largest counter-intelligence problem faced by Nato', recalled Murphy, 'the detailed information the tunnel provided on them was of special significance.' Of the telephone lines being tapped, twenty-five carried conversations between the GRU and intelligence units of the Intelligence Directorate of the Red Army in Germany (RU). As a result, Stopwatch/Gold identified more than 350 GRU and RU officers in East Germany, along with details on their organizations and agent operations. This proved invaluable for cross-checking and analysing information being provided by double agents being run by Lunn and Harvey. The lines also contained conversations between Red Army intelligence in Germany based at Wünsdorf and the General Staff of the Ministry of Defence in Moscow. Some of this provided surprising and welcome intelligence about GRU units in such far-flung places as the Tbilisi-based Transcaucasian district, covering the borders with Iran and Turkey.

The counter-intelligence directorate of the Red Army in Berlin, which was based in Potsdam, also produced rich material. From here its Director, Major-General Georgy Tsinev, ran networks of agents against Western intelligence units in West Berlin and West Germany. The work involved considerable liaison with both the KGB in Karlshorst and the East German Stasi, and generated hundreds of telephone calls. The tunnel taps revealed that the operations were 'a large, scattergun effort in which many low-level agents concentrated on exposing western agents'. The telephone also carried interesting conversations when the deputy chairman of the KGB and the chief of the KGB's Third Military Counter-Intelligence arrived from Moscow to conduct a personal investigation in Berlin of the running of the agent networks in the West. As David Murphy noted, the intelligence was used by Harvey and his counter-intelligence experts to check information provided by a Soviet defector from Potsdam.[7]

An additional bonus of Stopwatch/Gold was the wealth of material it provided on Soviet intercept operations. The tapping of lines between KGB Karlshorst and the Red Army signals directorate at Wünsdorf uncovered Soviet intercept operations specifically targeted on the radio transmissions of allied occupation forces in Berlin and West Germany, as well as the clandestine radio traffic of GRU agents at work in West Germany and other Nato countries. It included details on Soviet agent training techniques and facilities, the models and specifications of Soviet agents' radio sets, and information about the main radio station that directed the Soviet agent traffic involving the names of directing officers, the cover names of Soviet agents and co-operation between the GRU and KGB.

Each side was busy tapping into the other's communications, spies spying on spies, who in turn were playing the same game against their opponents. In this wilderness of mirrors, and amid the clutter of conversations being picked up on one of the target cables, Stopwatch/Gold got wind that the KGB was tapping an American cable near Potsdam. The evidence was oblique – a fragment of conversation here, an elliptical comment there – and the KGB officers using the line were highly security-conscious, but not quite aware enough to outwit the Stopwatch/Gold listeners. When the tunnel evidence was put alongside other CIA intelligence about the Karlshorst base, it provided enough hard intelligence about the KGB group at work, and the vehicles it was using, to pinpoint the cable involved and put an end to its use. This, along with the rest of Stopwatch/Gold's harvest, was, in David Murphy's words, 'a bonanza to Western counterintelligence specialists'.[8]

14

Fingers Crossed

'BIOGRAPHIC FILES ARE the heart of any intelligence service', writes the former CIA operative William Hood, 'and personal data on any possible target is eagerly collected by every intelligence agency.' But because intelligence officers themselves keep casual acquaintances at arm's length and are good at dissembling and role playing, they are among the toughest targets.[1] To any spy agency this is particularly true for the leader of the opposition. For the Stopwatch/Gold team this meant the head of the local KGB in Karlshorst, Lieutenant-General Yevgeny Petrovich Pitovranov.

In his mid-forties and with cover as senior counsellor at the Soviet embassy, Pitovranov had arrived in Berlin in August 1953 in the aftermath of the East German uprising. He had to rebuild the discredited Stasi, which had signally failed to predict the revolt. 'Things need fixing', he was told in no uncertain terms in Moscow. Pitovranov knew all about fixing. A hardened veteran of the Soviet system, he had been briefly imprisoned by Stalin before suddenly being promoted to head of foreign intelligence shortly before the dictator's death. Afterwards, he had miraculously survived the turmoil that swept the Kremlin and culminated in the death of the dreaded KGB head, Lavrenti Beria. Being a brother-in-law to Georgi Malenkov, Stalin's interim successor, undoubtedly helped.[2]

Pitovranov was not a man to require intricate lessons in telephone security. But like everyone else he had to make calls,

Allied listeners-in delighted in collecting intelligence about Yevgeny Pitovranov, the KGB station chief in Berlin. Rather than expose Blake, the Soviets continued to use the lines

however discreet. Besides, he was in no position to control what others said about him on lines being used in Berlin and elsewhere. Almost as soon as it began, Stopwatch/Gold was collating a file on him. Combined with other sources, such as personal surveillance, it still exists and was released by the CIA in 1995.[3] It provides a fascinating mix of personal and professional information on the local KGB chief gleaned from the intercepted telephone conversations of many people. This included Pitovranov himself. He and his wife, Elizaveta Pitovranova, talked to each other frequently by telephone, and from these conversations the Stopwatch/Gold eavesdroppers decided that the KGB chief was married to a person of 'listless and apathetic manner'. In October 1955, for example, after she flew to Moscow following the death of her mother, she showed little enthusiasm for returning to Berlin, despite endless telephone calls from her husband urging her to do so. She was also noticeably apathetic when a staff officer from Marshal Grechko's headquarters telephoned her about helping with some domestic transactions for Mrs Grechko. The dutiful wife Mrs Pitovranova certainly was not. All in all, concluded the listeners, she was 'either a sick person or one of negative personality'. Today, perhaps, she would be seen as a person of independent mind.

By contrast the analysts were impressed by Pitovranov himself. In December 1955 a Colonel Belov of the Red Army intelligence directorate in Berlin telephoned the KGB in Karlshorst to ask for Pitovranov's help with some agent. The Stopwatch/Gold team was once again listening in, carefully recording Belov's calls on the non-stop tape machines housed in the basement of the Rudow warehouse. It was clear that he was highly pleased with the KGB chief. He had made his decisions quickly, Belov told a colleague, and the operation concerned had gone off 'as quick as lightning'. In Karlshorst itself a subordinate of Pitovranov told a friend that the pressure of working in Berlin was like sitting on a powder barrel but was made easier by the fact that his boss was a fighter who backed up his staff. His seniors also held him in high regard and respect.

On only one occasion did the Stopwatch/Gold team pick up any criticism. This came from Major-General Dibrova, the commandant of the Soviet garrison in Berlin, and arose when he made the startling discovery that Pitovranov was planning a nightime wild boar hunting expedition using rifles with infra-red telescopic sights. Pitovranov, declared Dibrova to Lieutenant-General Kalyagin, Red Army liaison officer with the East German government, was 'a fool to introduce a system that reflected on his hunting ability'. Besides, he added almost as an afterthought, he might accidentally get some of the local population killed in the process.

The Pitovranov file contains detailed information on all his known movements, mostly the dates of flights to and from Moscow, but also trips made within the GDR to such cities as Karl-Marx-Stadt (Chemnitz) and the occasional visit to the KGB radio intercept station at Stahnsdorf, a village half-way between Berlin and Potsdam. It also lists his most important friends and colleagues, such as Marshal Grechko, with comments on their relationship. In all, the six typed pages of the CIA Pitovranov file add up to a mixed compendium of fact, gossip and speculation. This could easily be dismissed as at times amusing, sometimes interesting and frequently trivial, and certainly insignificant on the greater scale of the Cold War intelligence front, and probably a waste of time. Yet this would be a mistake. In the first place, every nugget of intelligence, however trivial, provided a piece of the jigsaw that eventually established the larger picture of Soviet intelligence in Berlin and elsewhere.

But equally important was its value as a check on information from other sources that could have enormous intelligence spin-off. The file, for example, records that Pitovranov paid an urgent visit to Stahnsdorf in January 1956, shortly after one of its radio intercept officers had defected to the West. Such defectors were often a valuable source of vital intelligence. But the CIA and SIS would need quickly to establish whether the defector was genuine: false defectors deliberately planted by the KGB, and fraudulent ones seeking to make money by claiming to be what they were not, were common in this urban swamp. The often mundane but accurate information provided by Stopwatch/Gold provided a rich databank of information against which to check their claims.

Pitovranov was far too careful to reveal that he knew anyone was listening in. He had been briefed on the tunnel soon after Blake revealed its secrets to Kondrashev early in 1954, and immediately placed the Rudow site under observation – discreetly enough, it appears, for Harvey's men not to pick it up. He also began some quiet investigation into the background of residents in the neighbourhood of the tap.

Then, late in 1955, when the tunnel was in full swing, KGB headquarters in Moscow sent out a team of technical specialists to Karlshorst under Vadim Goncharev. His task was twofold: first, to work with the signals directorate of Soviet forces in Berlin to tighten their communications security, and second, to provide 'cover' when the KGB and the Kremlin decided to move against Stopwatch/Gold. To ensure that the cover was foolproof, Goncharev was not told about the tunnel itself, and above all not about Blake. Instead, his Moscow bosses gave him just enough information about Western intercept operations to let him make an educated guess on his own that he should be looking for a tunnel. He knew about the KGB tap on the American cable in Potsdam. He could easily deduce that the opposition was doing the same with Soviet cables.

The first thing Goncharev did was to bustle around checking up on KGB telephone security. He was alarmed by what he uncovered. A random check of conversations revealed what he described as 'violations of the most elementary norms of security'. To make his point he had several of them taped and showed the results to Marshal Grechko. The head of Soviet forces in Germany was appalled. At first he was simply incredulous, finding it hard to believe that so much information could be gleaned from telephone chatter. But after listening to a sample tape he gave the appropriate instructions to his subordinate commanders to tighten telephone security.[4]

Goncharev then turned his attention to his more important

mission, and his team began searching for allied taps all along the Berlin sector border – anywhere where Soviet cables could be easily reached. This included the Alt-Glienicke area. Their initial explorations found nothing amiss until finally, early in 1956, closer checks using local telephone exchanges in different sectors of the city helped Goncharev pinpoint the exact location of the tunnel. Unaware that Pitovranov already knew the details, Goncharev excitedly told him of the discovery. Pitovranov could now move more overtly. He immediately went to Marshal Grechko, told him the 'news' and obtained his permission to create a special military signals company to locate and uncover any hostile taps on Soviet landlines in Berlin. The officers and enlisted men were carefully selected for hazardous duties, screened by the KGB and trained by Goncharev and his signals specialists. All that now remained was for the trap to be carefully sprung. For that, Pitovranov and Goncharev had patiently to await orders from the Kremlin.

★

Precisely when Khruschchev was told about the tunnel, and what precisely motivated him to pull the plug on it when he did, remain secrets still interred in the byzantine archives of the Kremlin. The Soviet leader revealed nothing himself about the decision and did not even mention the tunnel in his memoirs. But several events converged in April 1956 to explain his action. Most important was the continuing fall-out from his shattering denunciation of Stalin in his secret speech that February. To the West it sent a signal that a new and less hostile regime was in charge in Moscow. To dissident communist leaders, such as Marshal Tito in Yugoslavia, it held out the chance of reconciliation and return to the communist fold. Khrushchev enhanced both these aims in April when he abolished the Cominform, the international communist agency that had expelled Tito from its ranks back in 1948. As the successor to the Comintern, Cominform had also long been seen by the West as an arm of international Soviet propaganda.

Yet even as he sent out friendly signals with one hand, Khrushchev was under fierce pressure to demonstrate toughness with the other. With his attack on Stalin he had gone out on a limb against the wishes of the majority of his Politburo. To them, and to survive politically, he had to show he had not gone soft on the West. Challenging Stalin's legacy also seriously worried the Kremlin's puppet allies in the Warsaw Pact. Many owed their position to Stalin's support. Of nobody was this more true than of Walter Ulbricht, the East German dictator. The unloved German Democratic Republic was a fragile state, still unrecognized outside the Eastern bloc. Khrushchev knew it, and in September 1955 signed a treaty with Ulbricht promising to return as many powers to his regime as possible. What this meant in detail for Berlin was unclear. But against the destabilizing backdrop of his secret speech Khrushchev badly needed to assure Ulbricht of continuing support. Depicting West Berlin as a nest of American spies fitted perfectly into the game plan. Khrushchev was essentially reactive and opportunist. Exposing the tunnel would demonstrate to dubious allies, not to mention hardline factions in the Kremlin itself, that he was standing firm against the Americans. Done in the right way, exposure could deliver Khrushchev a much-needed propaganda victory. Looking back on events from almost fifty years later, Markus Wolf understood the need. 'In 1956, at the time of the 20th Party Congress', he recalled, 'there was an escalation of tension.'

None of this escaped the attention of the West. Admiral Arthur Radford, chairman of the American Joint Chiefs of Staff, told a meeting of the National Security Council chaired by Vice-President Richard Nixon at the end of 1955 that Berlin remained 'one area of the world where we can expect trouble in the near future'. Sitting at the table, Allen Dulles shared his anxiety. Tension was again rising in the Soviet zone of Germany, he told his colleagues, and 'further harassment and restrictions were likely to be imposed on West Berlin'. Two months later, in February 1956, Prime Minister Eden and President Eisenhower issued a joint public warning that any attack on West Berlin would be regarded as an attack on both Britain and the United States. In the spring of 1956 Khrushchev wished to demonstrate that he could still be tough. Berlin was the place to do it. So he gave the signal to the KGB to expose Stopwatch/Gold.[5]

Pitovranov choreographed a detailed plan for the 'accidental' discovery of the tunnel including 'spontaneous' statements of outrage by Marshal Grechko, Georgy Pushkin, the Soviet ambassador in East Berlin, and Pitovranov himself. All this was kept secret from the lower echelons of KGB. Other Soviet agencies in Berlin were also kept in the dark, as were the East Germans. They, too, were to believe that the tunnel's discovery was accidental.

Yet fate almost decreed otherwise. The first snowfall of winter revealed a fatal flaw in tunnel planning. It was the one story about Stopwatch/Gold that Allen Dulles was later prepared to tell in public, offering it as a warning about what can happen to even the most carefully laid plans. As the snow fell, a routine visual inspection above ground showed that it was melting because of the heat coming up from beneath. 'In no time at all a beautiful path was going to appear in the snow from West to East Berlin which any watchful Vopo couldn't help but notice', recalled Dulles. 'The heat was turned off and in short order refrigeration devices were installed in the tunnel. Fortunately it continued to snow and the path was quickly covered over . . .'[6]

The heavy rains that deluged Berlin in the spring handed Moscow the opportunity it needed to 'discover' the tunnel. They had caused severe flooding and many of the Soviet cables serving Karlshorst and Wünsdorf were short-circuiting. One of the cables being tapped, known to the Stopwatch/Gold team as FK 151, was so badly affected that on 17 April the Soviets had to cut out a defective stretch and replace it with a 3,000 metre length of temporary cable. FK 151 was a vital part of the Soviet early warning system, carrying the air warning link between Moscow and Marshal Grechko's headquarters at Wünsdorf. Its traffic was so important that while it was being repaired messages were diverted on to another of the cables being tapped, FK 150.

But then this, too, began to have problems. Exasperated, the head of the Wünsdorf signal centre, Lieutenant-Colonel Vyunik, placed an urgent call to his opposite number at KGB Karlshorst, insisting that the line be fixed by the next morning, Sunday 22 April.

Listening in, the CIA and SIS eavesdroppers overheard the Soviets trying to cope with the crisis. Independently their agents inside the East German telephone office confirmed the story. The crisis obviously posed a serious risk to the tunnel, so Lunn sent an urgent warning message to Broadway. Joe Evans rememberd the alert. 'We received a warning from Berlin that flooding threatened the tunnel', he recalled. 'From flooding could come faults on phone lines we tapped and if this occurred – as it did – East German phone workers could find the chamber while searching for faults.'[7]

In Berlin, Harvey decided to reassure himself that all was well and that the emergency Soviet work on the cables was not disguising an attack on the tunnel. While the press was headlining the fairy-tale wedding of actress Grace Kelly to Prince Rainier of Monaco, Harvey's men inspected the tap chamber on 19 April. All was in order. Harvey passed on the news to Lunn. Neither had any reason to suspect that anything was out of the ordinary. None the less they remained vigilant. All precautions had been taken, Harvey reported to Truscott in Frankfurt on 20 April, 'including the primary one of crossing fingers'.[8]

But superstition was not enough. Though neither Lunn nor Harvey knew it, everything was about to change. Stopwatch/ Gold was set to emerge into the harsh, bright light of worldwide publicity.

15

'It's Gone, John'

'MOST INTELLIGENCE OPERATIONS have a limited span of usefulness', declared Allen Dulles. 'The difficult decision is when to
taper off and when to stop.'[1] This assumes the master spy is in
control. But for Stopwatch/Gold the decision was in the hands
of the enemy. Shortly before one o'clock on the morning of 22
April, a Sunday, a team of between forty and fifty men from
Goncharev's special signal unit under the command of a Captain
Bartash arrived at the exact point on the east side of the
Schönefelder Chaussee traversed by the tunnel. They were
directly above the tap chamber just inches below the surface.
Piling out of their trucks and wielding picks and shovels, they
began to dig up the road.

Over at the Rudow warehouse the CIA watchers immediately
spotted them through their night-vision binoculars. Following
the pre-arranged security procedures they promptly alerted Bill
Harvey via the switchboard in the CIA office on the Clayallee.
Hurriedly throwing on his clothes, Harvey dashed out to
Rudow. But first he telephoned Hugh Montgomery. 'I was at
home fast asleep when his call woke me up', recalled
Montgomery. 'All he said was "We've got a problem" so I flung
on my clothes and went over.' When he got out to Rudow,
Harvey told him to help the duty linguists monitor the conver-
sations being intercepted on the engineering circuits as well as

anything being picked up by the microphone still installed in the tap chamber. 'I was sitting there,' said Montgomery, 'listening in on the headphones'.

By this time Harvey was already standing by a tape machine. Every now and again he ordered it to be stopped so that the linguists could interpret for him. The conversations were in both German and Russian. This was not just front-seat curiosity on Harvey's part. He was straining to catch any evidence from the idle chatter of the diggers that the Soviets already knew about the tunnel, and hence to establish whether or not it had been betrayed. Even as Stopwatch/Gold was unravelling, Harvey's counter-intelligence instincts were fully on the alert. In the background, through the static, he heard shovelling, the noise of falling debris, passing traffic, a barking dog, even a rooster crowing.

After about fifty minutes coughing and panting the Soviet team uncovered the top of the tap chamber. None of them had been told by the KGB about the tunnel and they still thought they were searching for a flood-damaged cable, so they failed to realize what they had found and assumed it was a manhole covering a repeater point (an automatic re-transmitting device) in the cable system. They continued digging. After another hour they uncovered the tap cables and could see them leading down through a trapdoor in the floor of the chamber. Still they were unconcerned and, even as they worked, the taps continued. Over in the warehouse Harvey continued his vigil. Majors Alpatov and Vyunik, in the signals centres at Karlshorst and Wünsdorf respectively, continued to talk about the air warning communications system with Moscow and the troubles they were having with cable FK 150. Harvey detected nothing to show they were aware of the tap.

By now the hidden microphone was beginning to pick up fragments of conversation. The Soviet specialists had been joined by East German telephone repair men. Harvey's eavesdroppers heard one of them suggest that the chamber might have something to do with the Berlin city sewer system. Should they obtain a plan of the system, he asked. He was brusquely snubbed by a Soviet officer. They already had the sewer map, he replied curtly, and it was obvious that this was something different.

Still, however, the digging team had no idea what they had uncovered. Was it something built by the Nazis during the war, wondered one of them. Then, at about 3.30 a.m., the Soviet contingent abruptly withdrew. Through their night-vision binoculars the CIA watchers saw them pile into their vehicles and disappear down the Schönefelder Chaussee, leaving behind a handful of East Germans, one or two guard dogs and improvised barricades around the site. It had finally sunk in to the Soviet diggers that they had unearthed something major. They needed higher authority before proceeding any further.

Soon after they left, Vyunik in Wünsdorf telephoned Alpatov at his KGB apartment in Karlshorst. Had he spoken to the head of GSFG signals, General Dudakov, asked Vyunik. Yes, replied Alpatov, adding that he was actually in the middle of getting dressed to make it back to his office. 'Telephone me when you get there', requested Vyunik. 'When we speak we must do so carefully. We know what the matter is, so we will speak carefully.' Listening in, Harvey realized this was the first sign that the Soviets had begun to guess what they had found.

Two hours after Captain Bartash's team withdrew, they were back again, this time accompanied by the deputy chief of the lines department from Wünsdorf, Lieutenant-Colonel Zolochko. Soon after they arrived, Bill Harvey heard the words 'the cable is tapped' picked up on the microphone. By now several more high-ranking Soviet officials had arrived, alerted to the fact that something extraordinary was going on. They even brought a motion picture camera team along. From now on every stage of the operation's exposure was carefully recorded on film. It was at about this time, too, that Markus Wolf and Ernst Wollweber rolled up in their battered old Volkswagen.

The diggers had still not penetrated beyond the tap chamber. They were being careful. It might be booby-trapped. Yet, remarkably, the full scale of the discovery had still not dawned on them. Some thought they had uncovered an abandoned tap, and even though they spotted it, none of them recognized the microphone for what it was. Harvey continued to follow their talk as they speculated wildly about what they had found. How could the cuts have been made in the cables to attach the tap lines without anyone noticing, wondered one of the Soviets. 'Everyone must have been drunk', suggested one of the Germans familiar with the habits of his vodka-prone comrades. Another demonstrated how deeply in the dark the diggers were. 'They themselves must have some means of entering this place, but naturally it's highly improbable that they have constructed a passage for getting from here to there,' he remarked.

By now it was 11.30 a.m. on 22 April. Digging had been under way for ten hours. Captain Bartash's men still did not know they were dealing with a tunnel. Then, at quarter to twelve, one of the Germans shouted, 'The box is an entry to a shaft.' They had finally hacked a small hole near the still intact trapdoor and were peering through into the lower part of the chamber. Reassured by now that there was no booby trap, they removed the hinges of the door and clambered down. One of the first things they saw was the padlock that secured the trap-door from below. It was of British origin. The next thing they encountered was the massive steel door sealing the tap chamber off from the pre-amplification chamber. They were unable to open it. Instead, they broke through the wall with their picks and drills to reveal an impressive array of technology.

They were stunned. 'Fantastic! Look at that! It goes all the way under the highway', exclaimed one. 'I am speechless', declared another. Yet another cried out, 'It's a complete installation, a telephone exchange.' One of them marvelled at the sophisticated equipment and the careful planning involved. 'It must have cost a pretty penny', he remarked. One of the Germans observed, 'How neatly and tidily they have done it', but another colleague was less impressed. 'What a filthy trick', he spluttered, 'and where you would least expect it'. Meanwhile the Soviet film kept rolling.

An East German border guard points at Harvey's hurriedly written note marking the sector border

Harvey was still listening in as the microphone picked up these exclamations of shock and amazement. So far he had listened fascinated but fairly detached. But as the Soviet team began to break its way into the pre-amplification chamber he suddenly sprang into action. 'Find Dasher', he shouted to Montgomery, referring to General Charles L. Dasher, the American commander in Berlin. Montgomery was to ask the general's permission to prime and if necessary detonate the explosive charges in the tunnel.

After a hectic search Montgomery finally located Dasher at a reception being given at the Wannsee Yacht Club for General Maxwell Taylor, the US Army's Chief of Staff, who was on an official visit to Berlin. 'He wasn't at all pleased to be interrupted', remembered Montgomery, 'but I insisted.' The irate general gradually calmed down as Montgomery explained the problem. 'Might any of the Russians get killed', asked Dasher when he had finished. 'Possibly', responded Montgomery. 'Then the answer's No', replied Dasher, 'I don't want to start World War Three.' Montgomery relayed Dasher's veto back to Harvey by telephone. 'I think Harvey expected that', surmised Montgomery. Instead, the CIA Berlin chief ordered sandbags and barbed wire to be placed in the tunnel where it crossed the sector border. On top of the improvised barrier he put up a crude hand-lettered sign. 'You are now entering the American sector', it read. A few yards further on he ordered his men to set up a .50 calibre heavy machine gun. It was not loaded, merely a deterrent. Harvey menacingly crouched down behind it.

At about 3 o'clock he and Montgomery heard footsteps moving down through the tunnel towards them. There was a small dip in the tunnel floor obscuring Harvey's view. He pulled back the bolt. Its noise echoed loudly along the tunnel. The footsteps stopped, then after a short pause retreated back into the darkness. Half an hour later the Soviets cut the tap cables and dismantled the microphone. 'It's gone, John', muttered one of the listening American linguists. His words were the last to be captured on the transcript as the microphone went dead. After eleven months and eleven days Stopwatch/Gold had completed its work.[2]

16

Caught Red-Handed

THE MOMENT HE realized the tunnel was blown, Harvey alerted CIA headquarters in Frankfurt. By now Lucien Truscott had been replaced by the OSS veteran and wartime parachutist Tracy Barnes. 'Every morning', recalled his widow years later, 'Tracy got up and went to war.' Barnes had capped his Second World War exploits by working with Allen Dulles in Berne, where he met the grieving widow of the former Italian Foreign Minister Count Galeazzo Ciano – hanged in 1944 by his father-in-law Mussolini – and charmed her into handing over his diaries. Since then, he had enthusiastically waged Cold War against the communists from within the CIA.

Two versions exist of what happened after Harvey's call reached Frankfurt. One has Barnes entertaining the CIA's Deputy Director of Intelligence, Robert Amory, who was on a fact-finding European visit. The two men jumped into a Mercedes and rushed up the autobahn to Bonn to break the news to the American ambassador, James Conant. As decreed earlier by Dulles, Conant had not been let into the secret of Stopwatch/Gold. But by the time Barnes and Amory arrived he had already heard from Berlin of the drama unfolding at Alt-Glienicke. 'Well, fellows', he greeted them laughing, 'looks like you got your hands caught in the cookie jar. Tell me all about it.'[1] According to the second version, told by Barnes's widow,

Barnes was in Switzerland when the call came through. 'Tracy was wild', she recalled. 'He woke me up and said "This is serious" and roared off to Bonn to tell the ambassador.' When told the news, Conant said simply, 'I like cops and robbers, but I don't like getting caught.'[2]

Either way, Conant was not the only one eager to hear the news. The tunnel might have gone, but its unearthing was far from the end of the story. The events of Sunday 22 April sparked an international row, unveiled an orchestrated Cold War propaganda spectacle, set off urgent internal inquests by both CIA and SIS into the possibilities of treachery and initiated a decades-long debate about the significance of Stopwatch/Gold that lasted until after the collapse of the Soviet Union itself.

The Stopwatch/Gold planners had assumed that the Soviets would keep quiet about the tunnel rather than suffer a loss of face by admitting that the West had outwitted them with such an impressive operation. So Moscow's response took them aback. Within hours of the tunnel's discovery the Soviet ambassador in East Berlin, Georgy Pushkin, delivered a strong official protest to General Dasher. Two days later Moscow mobilized the press. At about 7 p.m. on the evening of 24 April calls went out to journalists in Berlin inviting them to a press conference in the cinema of the Red Army officers' club in Karlshorst.

Such a rare flash of Soviet openness sparked immediate curiosity and stimulated a mad rush to get there. At Karlshorst the news-hungry journalists were greeted by Colonel Ivan Kotsiuba, the Soviet military commandant in the city. After warmly welcoming his guests from the West he revealed the discovery of the 'American spy tunnel'. He then invited them all on a guided tour. Spearheaded by Soviet military police on motor bikes, a convoy of vehicles dashed at breakneck speed through the darkening Berlin evening to Alt-Glienicke. Here the scene was lit by floodlights. 'Come, gentleman, follow me', said the smiling Kotsiuba, disappearing down the hole. 'Look', he said, 'almost German workmanship – but not done by Germans.'[3] He allowed the gaping journalists to walk down the tunnel as far as

In this carefully posed photograph a lieutenant-colonel in the Red Army examines some of the Western technology used in the Berlin tunnel

the hastily improvised barbed wire barrier and Harvey's notice marking the beginning of the American sector.

'The chamber near the Soviet end of the tunnel', marvelled the *New York Times'* correspondent, 'looked like the communications center of a battleship.' Talking to an American official in Bonn, one senior British diplomat noted that the Americans were happy to play up the tunnel as an example of Cold War toughness. 'At the moment', he informed London, 'they are laughing it off as a good joke on the Soviets.'[4] Over the NBC radio network broadcaster Alex Dreier voiced another good joke. Why didn't the Americans open up a tourist entrance at their end of the tunnel and cash in on the publicity? 'Step up, one and all', he laughed. 'Only a quarter. See modern espionage in electronic form and all underground, and who knows? Perhaps you'll meet an occasional foreign tourist.'[5]

★

While the American media hailed the tunnel for its ingenuity and lauded the CIA for at last outwitting the Soviets, the KGB unleashed a cascade of anti-CIA propaganda. In his guided tour Kotsiuba had pointed his finger firmly at the Americans. A few weeks later Moscow produced a widely distributed booklet entitled *Caught Red-Handed*. It was lavishly illustrated with photographs taken by the Soviet cameramen and contained a sketch of the site showing the path of the tunnel between the Schönefelder Chaussee and Rudow: damning evidence, it proclaimed, of the CIA's use of West Berlin as an espionage base against the peace-loving East. Even communist China jumped on the bandwagon by posting photographs of the tunnel in shops and factories and reporting gleefully that they were provoking 'lively discussion' among their workers.

But the real KGB target was the host of other 'criminal activities' denounced in the booklet. The list included over twenty agents caught between 1952 and 1956 inside the USSR itself. They had now, noted the text with satisfaction, been 'rendered harmless'. It also contained details of the James Bond-style equipment they were alleged to have used: miniature radio transmitters, pencils using luminous ink for writing at night, and fountain pen pistols firing poison-filled bullets. The agents were all declared to have belonged to the Gehlen organization. For years its real and imagined links with the CIA had been providing a prime target for the KGB.

During the Second World War General Reinhard Gehlen headed the Abwehr's Foreign Armies East section, collecting intelligence about the Soviet Union. In 1945 he turned over his wares to the Americans, who set him up in a base at Pullach, outside Munich. From here he ran extensive operations into Eastern Europe and the Soviet Union. Gehlen was always controversial. The value of his intelligence was disputed and his agency was inevitably tainted by its Nazi past. Particularly after the 1953 uprising this was seized on by the East Germans, who targeted his agency with an unremitting smear campaign and even offered a million Deutschmarks reward for his capture, dead or alive. They also bent all their efforts to penetrate his agency. Far too often they succeeded, which was why both the CIA and SIS kept him firmly at arm's length. Such episodes were invariably exploited to the full for their propaganda advantage.

One such incident had occurred in December 1953, just as the first CIA–SIS planning meeting was taking place at Carlton Gardens. Major Werner Haase was a Gehlen officer in West Berlin. One night he was reconnoitring a possible route for a secret telephone cable across a canal that ran along the sector border, a device that would enable him to maintain contact with his agents in East Berlin now that overground courier routes were becoming increasingly dangerous. 'Under cover of darkness', recalled Gehlen, 'he proposed to feed the cable along the canal using a toy steamboat, helped by an agent from East Berlin on the other side.' What Major Haase did not know was that his agent had been turned by the Stasi. In mid-operation Ulbricht's secret policemen swooped and arrested him. They later paraded him in a show trial and he was given life imprisonment. It was a vivid reminder to the Stopwatch/Gold planners, if one was needed, of the hazards of dealing with Gehlen's men.[6]

By the early 1950s Gehlen was effectively head of West German intelligence. The regaining of sovereignty by the Federal Republic meant that in 1956 it could finally create its own official foreign intelligence agency. On 1 April that year Gehlen's organization formally became the BND – the Bundesnachrichtendienst, or foreign intelligence service. This was just three weeks before the tunnel was blown. Moscow's decision to pull the plug provided Khrushchev with a potent propaganda weapon against the new Federal Republic.

The KGB would always claim that Gehlen had been deeply involved in the planning and execution of the Berlin tunnel. The suggestion has been widely repeated in many other sources, including biographies of Gehlen and histories of the CIA. But no evidence exists to back it up and those most closely in the know in the CIA have strenuously denied it. Most revealingly of all, Gehlen himself noticeably refrained from making any claim of involvement in Stopwatch/Gold in his published 1972 memoirs. Never a modest man, he would surely have bid for some of the credit had he been any way involved. In fact, he does not even refer to it.[7]

Denouncing the Gehlen connection was not the only object of Soviet propaganda. Praising KGB skill was another. Soon a vivid account began to circulate in the world's press of the Soviets descending on the tunnel as the hapless Americans fled the scene. 'On a table in the recreation chamber [*sic*] a coffee percolator was still bubbling', wrote the popular historian E.H. Cookridge in his vividly coloured biography of Gehlen.[8] Versions of this story have circulated ever since, but it is a myth. Harvey's men spotted the Soviet search party on the Schönefelder Chaussee even before it began digging up the road, and Goncharev's team took a full fourteen hours fully to uncover the taps. No one working in the tunnel was so surprised that they fled leaving the coffee pot on. There was not even a coffee pot in the tunnel: refreshments were always taken in the warehouse building.

Equally misleading were sketches of the tunnel that appeared in the East German press within days of the tunnel's discovery. These showed it originating in the motor pool garage or power generating plant and not, as was actually the case, in the 'radar station' itself. This was either a genuine mistake or, more likely, a deliberate error to conceal the fact that the KGB had an inside source on the tunnel plans, in the shape of George Blake.[9]

Here, too, another myth has taken hold – that it was intelligence gleaned from Stopwatch/Gold itself that first alerted SIS to Blake's treachery.[10] But the notion that the KGB would have discussed Blake, however indirectly, over lines that they knew were being tapped by SIS stretches credulity. Furthermore, those in the CIA who examined the tunnel material for counter-intelligence material never saw any evidence of this kind.

★

Nowhere in Soviet propaganda about the Berlin tunnel was there any reference to the British. Yet SIS involvement was glaringly apparent to anyone who went into it. One of those taken on Colonel Kotsiuba's underground tour in Alt-Glienicke was the Berlin-based Charles Hargrove, of *The Times* of London. 'Your correspondent was given the opportunity today to climb down a ladder into the tunnel', he reported to British readers the next day. 'The roadside on the way to East Berlin airport this afternoon resembled an archaeological site after exciting new finds . . . The vital part is a short section near the East Berlin end in which is housed a complete telephone switchboard of a current British manufacture . . . fluorescent lighting, fire extinguishers, and other equipment in the switchboard section all bear familiar British trade marks.' But, he added, the Soviets had not yet accused the British authorities of complicity and maintained that the whole tunnel was recognizably American work.[11] The newspaper then fell remarkably silent about the British fingerprints at the scene. Apart from this initial report and one or two subsequent small snippets about Soviet protests to the Americans, Britain's premier national broadsheet abruptly dropped the story.

The Berlin tunnel is exposed as 'an imperialist plot' while Soviet leaders Bulganin (at the microphone) and Khrushchev are on an official visit to the UK. Here, Prime Minister Anthony Eden (arms crossed) greets them at Victoria Station just four days before the Soviets 'stumble' on the tunnel

The explanation was simple. Even as Captain Bartash's men in Berlin were discovering the British-made padlock on the tap chamber trapdoor, Nikita Khrushchev, First Secretary of the Communist Party of the USSR, and Marshal Nikolai Bulganin, the Soviet Prime Minister, were asleep in their beds at Chequers as guests of the British Prime Minister, Sir Anthony Eden. There was a heavy political investment at stake and no one was prepared to rock the diplomatic boat.

The Soviet leaders had arrived at Portsmouth four days before on the Soviet cruiser *Ordzhonikidze* for an official state visit first proposed by Eden at the Geneva conference the year before. It was trumpeted in the British press as heralding the beginning of a new and more hopeful era of *détente* following the death of

Stalin. By contrast with the grim and brooding Georgian, the jovial Khrushchev and his smiling prime minister showed to the world a more human face of the Soviet Union. They stayed at Claridge's Hotel, made sightseeing tours of such tourist spots as Westminster Abbey, St Paul's Cathedral, the Tower of London and the Royal Festival Hall, and solemnly laid a wreath on the cenotaph in Whitehall in memory of the soldiers of both nations who had died in 'common struggles for peace and security' in the two world wars. They also laid a wreath on the grave of Karl Marx in Highgate Cemetery. There were formal dinners at 10 Downing Street and lunches in the magnificent Painted Hall of the Royal Naval College at Greenwich and the City of London's Mansion House. They flew to Birmingham and to Edinburgh, where they toured Holyrood House and Edinburgh Castle.

The only hitch came at a dinner hosted by the Labour Party, when the party leader, Hugh Gaitskell, presented the Soviet leaders with a list of Social Democrats imprisoned in Eastern Europe. Truculently, Khrushchev asked why he should care what happened to enemies of the working class. 'God forgive you', shouted an emotional George Brown, Gaitskell's chief lieutenant. Unused to the robust exchanges of British socialists, the offended Soviet leader remarked the next day that if he lived in Britain he would be a Tory.[12]

But this was just a hiccup in an otherwise harmonious visit. The highlight, which symbolized the hopes for peace in the steely Cold War world, was the visit by these heirs of Stalin to Her Majesty the Queen. After leaving Chequers on the afternoon of 22 April they were driven by car to Windsor. Here, in warm spring sunshine, they were greeted by a chorus of cheers from the waiting crowd before disappearing inside for an hour's royal audience. They then presented gifts to all the royal family: a sable fur wrap for the Queen herself, a horse for the Duke of Edinburgh, a pony for Prince Charles, and a bear cub, Nikki, for Princess Anne – later to be cared for at London Zoo.

Even as they were on their way Bill Harvey was pulling back the bolt on his machine-gun, the taps were being cut, the microphone was disconnected, and the Stopwatch/Gold secret was well and truly out of the bag. A full-scale diplomatic disaster loomed. But the Kremlin decreed otherwise. Khrushchev was fully briefed on the tunnel by the KGB and had already given his orders. The diplomatic and propaganda responses were firmly in place. Within hours of the tunnel's discovery Moscow issued detailed instructions to Berlin for the handling of the press. They included the unambiguous order: 'Despite the fact that the tunnel contains English equipment, direct all accusations in the press against the Americans only.'[13]

Bulganin and Khrushchev remained in Britain for five days after the unmasking of Stopwatch/Gold, plenty of time to embarrass their hosts had they wished to do so. They did not. Before leaving London the two Soviet leaders held a press conference at the Central Hall in Westminster attended by more than 400 British and foreign journalists. There was no hint of anything untoward; in fact the mood was distinctly upbeat. A smiling Bulganin announced that Eden had accepted an invitation to visit the Soviet Union as soon as he could. Certainly, admitted the Soviet Prime Minister, there had been differences and 'sharp moments' during the talks. East–West relations contained many difficult issues. But, he assured them, he and Mr Khrushchev were returning to Moscow full of friendly feelings towards the British people and government. 'The main thing we have achieved', he said, 'is greater confidence between the Soviet Union and Britain . . . Neither the British people nor the British Government want war.'[14] By implication, of course, others did. Bulganin was trying hard to drive a wedge between London and Washington.

Such benevolent talk dutifully followed the diplomatic plot. But to those in the know about SIS operations, a short phrase used by Bulganin undoubtedly raised a wry smile. Alongside the 'sharp moments', declared Bulganin, the talks had also encountered 'certain underwater rocks'. This might have been a deliberately coded reference to the excavations in Berlin. But it more likely referred to the ill-fated mission just a few days before of

Commander Lionel 'Buster' Crabb, a frogman sent by SIS to examine the hull of the *Ordzhonikidze* in Portsmouth Harbour. After a couple of dives Crabb failed to resurface, thus setting off panic and a frantic cover-up. Even as Bulganin spoke, SIS was still ignorant of Crabb's fate. It was not until after the Soviets had left Britain that Moscow officially protested about his exploits and that his disappearance was publicly admitted in Parliament. Crabb's headless torso was washed up near Chichester Harbour a year later. But whether Bulganin was hinting at Stopwatch/Gold or at 'Buster' Crabb, or possibly both, he and Khrushchev allowed neither of these two SIS operations to spoil the diplomatic party.[15]

17

'A Gangster Act'

In Washington, Allen Dulles remained tight-lipped. But behind the scenes he was jubilant at the favourable publicity the tunnel had won for the CIA. 'Money Well Spent', headlined the *Stamford Advocate* from Connecticut in noting that the news from Berlin should calm Congressional fears. 'What the Agency ultimately got', writes Burton Hersh in *The Old Boys*, his study of the American élite and the CIA, 'was publicity, priceless publicity, the kind that paved Allen's way to friction-free appearances before Congress.'[1]

As for Eisenhower, he was sorry to have lost the tunnel as a source of intelligence but had always been prepared for the inevitable. None the less, his staff secretary Andrew Goodpaster, the White House link with the CIA, recalled that discovery of the tunnel changed relations between the agency and the President. 'I think he felt that there had been carelessness that drew the attention of the East Germans. [He] responded by tightening White House supervision of all CIA activities encroaching on foreign sovereignty.'[2] No one in the American press, which was far more respectful of the White House in the 1950s than later, even suggested that Eisenhower had known about the tunnel. At his next press conference he was asked not a single question about it.

★

Back in Berlin, Moscow's rapid denunciation of the CIA was quickly picked up by its obedient East German satellite. The Ulbricht regime had said nothing at first about Stopwatch/Gold. But then it announced that a special commission had investigated the affair and proved it was an undoubted act of American espionage. The main target of Ulbricht's campaign was West Berlin, which from now until the building of the wall in 1961 came under a sustained communist attack in an effort to break its links with the West. The main thrust of the offensive was to denounce the city as a NATO base and nest of American spies and saboteurs.

East Berlin papers described the tunnel as 'an international scandal' that breached all the norms of international law and violated not just international telecommunications treaties but also the sovereignty of the GDR itself. The SED (communist) party newspaper *Neues Deutschland* characterized it as 'a gangster act' of the American secret service and produced a cartoon showing a garden divided into two separate halves. One, labelled 'Democratic Sector', is full of flowers. The other, a barren piece of land, is marked by a molehill topped by a flag with a dollar sign. In the 'Democratic Sector' a strong arm is pulling out of a hole a mole wearing earphones marked 'U.S.', army trousers with plugs and pliers showing from the pocket, and a US Army cap bearing the words 'Espionage'. The cartoon is captioned 'Do Not Burrow in Other People's Yards'. Another communist paper, the *Neue Zeit*, declared that there was no word strong enough to brand 'such wickedness'. The tunnel, it claimed, was a feature of West Berlin's misuse as a Nato base and it called for all-German talks about the future of the city, and 'not underground trenches in the cold war'.[3] The mayor of East Berlin, Fritz Ebert, invited his opposite numbers in the West to see the American spy tunnel for themselves.

The West Berlin response was exceptionally robust. The two halves of the city had long been bitter ideological enemies. Neither the mayor of West Berlin nor other West German officials had had any inkling of the tunnel and they were all as surprised as the international press by its discovery. But Willy Brandt, the most powerful figure in the city's Social Democratic Party, and soon to become world-famous as its embattled mayor when the wall went up, seized the opportunity to make propaganda of his own. He would happily visit the tunnel, he said, provided he could do so in the company of four political prisoners in the Soviet zone, whom he named.

Most were Social Democrats. But one, Lieutenant-General Robert Bialek, was an important East German defector from 1953 who had once run the East German state security service. Housed by SIS in the British sector in a flat fitted with automatic locks and steel window shutters, he had been kidnapped back to the East just a few weeks before. Since then the British had made repeated protests to the Soviet authorities in the East. They denied all knowledge of him.[4]

On Saturday 28 April at 11 a.m. Brandt ostentatiously arrived by car at the Brandenburg Gate. Not surprisingly, the four political prisoners were not there. After some fruitless discussions with East German officials Brandt returned to his office in the West of the city, declaring that he hoped they would be delivered to him there at some later date. The whole spectacle was witnessed by a crowd of camera-popping West German journalists. Most gave Brandt's stage-managed performance massive and favourable publicity. The one notable exception was the *Frankfurter Allgemeine*, which at the time was pushing for a united and neutral Germany. It published an angry editorial on the tunnel demanding that Germans should no longer tolerate the waging of a Russian–American Cold War on German soil.[5]

Meanwhile, the Ulbricht regime rapidly organized propaganda tours of the site at Alt-Glienicke, which quickly became the most popular tourist destination in the city. 'It has been turned into a major tourist attraction', noted British observers stationed at the Olympic Stadium, 'and scarcely a day passes without delegations of some sort or another being conducted through it.'[6] In the first week alone more than 2,000 visitors descended the shaft on the Schönefelder Chaussee. A mobile

Wilhelm Pieck, East German President (centre), gazes down at the targeted cables and the tap chamber beneath

snack bar serving beer and sausages did a thriving business. Factory delegations arrived daily by bus to see the work of 'the American imperialists'. Afterwards they wrote comments in a visitors' book to record their indignation. American reporters in particular were welcomed and fêted.

So were trade unionists from the West. One of them, John Forster, of the British Metal Workers Union, was reported as saying that he was very hurt to find British products in the tunnel. He was convinced, according to the report, that if the British metal workers knew what had happened to their products they would have been as angry as he was. 'The British working class', he was quoted as saying, 'did not allow itself to be misused to cause damage to the workers in the Soviet Union and the DDR.'[7] This was one of the very few references to British involvement in Stopwatch/Gold. Even then, East German papers echoed the Soviet line. References to British equipment, they argued, were probably attempts by the Americans to conceal their own responsibility.

By the end of June 1956 the tunnel had served its propaganda purpose. The tours were stopped, the entrance blocked up, the Schönefelder Chaussee resurfaced. Life in Alt-Glienicke returned to normal. Harvey's men emptied the tunnel of its equipment and at that end too it was bricked off. The warehouse and other buildings remained in place, however, and were used by the American army until the 1980s. Then they, too, fell into disuse.

★

With both the communist and American press alike accepting the tunnel as a CIA operation, Peter Lunn found it hard to keep quiet. In London some of those at SIS headquarters most deeply involved in Stopwatch/Gold, such as Andrew King, urged strongly that the British role should be made public. But this was firmly vetoed by the Foreign Office, anxious to keep relations with Moscow on an even keel.

Instead, Lunn assembled all his staff at the Olympic Stadium and told the entire story of the tunnel from its inception to its end. It was an emotional affair. One of those present was George Blake. Lunn made it clear, recalled Blake, 'that this had been essentially an SIS idea and his own to boot. American participation had been limited to providing most of the money and the facilities. They were, of course, also sharing in the product.'[8]

After this Lunn began to lose interest in Berlin and made it known he would like a transfer. That summer SIS obliged by moving him to Bonn as head of station. But he never forgot Stopwatch/Gold and his lectures on the operation became the staple diet of new recruits to the service for many years afterwards. His place in Berlin was taken by Robert Dawson, who had headed one of its sub-stations. Blake, happily ensconced in his SIS office at the Olympic Stadium, and still betraying his colleagues to the KGB, remained in post.

But one secret unknown to Blake remained undisclosed until now. There was a plan for a second Berlin tunnel. It was, as might be predicted, the brainchild of the inventive John Wyke. Even as the first tunnel was beginning to deliver its potent harvest of intelligence, Wyke raised the question that others were already asking. What if the Soviets discovered it and cut short its product? Was it worthwhile putting another in place, both to fill the gap and to exploit other lines? Lunn approved the plan and it went to Broadway for discussion. In the meantime Wyke scouted out the ground in Berlin. To spread the risk, this one would be in the British sector, and the site would depend on the very limited areas of the city where the border ran close to known cables being used by the opposition.

In the end a suitable site was found on the Stresemannstrasse, close to the Potsdamer Platz. Here, in a small alleyway just yards inside the British sector off the Wilhelmstrasse, Lunn and his agents located a small scrapyard. From here only a short tunnel was needed to reach the closest Soviet cable, a remnant of the old Wehrmacht system that had serviced Göring's Air Ministry building and now functioned as the headquarters for all East German government ministers. Tentatively the project was given the code name Bronze.

But in the end this second Berlin tunnel never got beyond the drawing board. Even though the scrapyard, with its coming and going of vehicles, offered excellent cover, the problem of where to put the excavated earth could not be solved. The exposure of the first tunnel finally killed it off when it was realized that the Soviets would almost certainly take special measures to protect other cables. In the aftermath of the Crabb affair Eden wanted no more embarrassments with Moscow. Nor did Eisenhower welcome the idea of dealing with yet further allegations about the violation of Soviet territory.[9]

18

Tunnel Visions

Soviet discovery of Stopwatch/Gold sparked an immediate inquiry by the CIA and SIS into the possibility of betrayal. But a three-month analysis both of the cable traffic and of conversations picked up by the microphone in the tap chamber, as well as a review of the visual surveillance carried out from the warehouse at Rudow, concluded that the forcible closure of the operation was not the result of penetration, or of a security violation, or of the testing of the lines by the Soviets or the East Germans. In Berlin the Stopwatch/Gold team came to the same conclusion. 'We didn't dream it had been betrayed', Hugh Montgomery recalled. 'All the evidence suggested it was random. There'd been flooding and short-circuiting on the lines and they'd dug at several points along the way. Also the Soviets took care to send in the East Germans. So far as we were concerned, it was all an accident.'[1]

With that, the normal processing of the intelligence was given the go-ahead. The tunnel was no longer producing taps. But an enormous backlog of tapes had piled up in London and Washington awaiting analysis. It took another two years to sift until the work was formally closed at the end of September 1958. By that time whatever had been captured on tape was largely out of date and no longer of much value.

The loss of the tunnel was a blow, but not the catastrophe it might have been even two years earlier. Although *détente* was in the air, this was not the reason. The nuclear arms race was fully under way and Washington and London were still demanding advance warning of Soviet attack. More relevant was that a new source of intelligence had just come on stream.

Barely a week after Colonel Kotsiuba gleefully led the press through the tunnel in Berlin, a United States Air Force transport plane touched down at Lakenheath airfield, a Second World War RAF base in Suffolk being used by the Americans. Its cargo was hurriedly unloaded into a remote hangar on the edge of the airfield. Here American technicians specially flown in two days before assembled what looked like a long-nosed glider with a razor-like tail. Painted black, with no identification marks, its wing span twice the length of its fuselage, and built out of light-weight titanium, this was the famous U-2 spy plane. Built in California by Lockheed at the CIA's request, it was equipped with state-of-the-art high-resolution cameras and designed for high-speed, high-level reconnaissance flights at more than 70,000 feet over the Soviet Union. The cover story claimed the plane was to be used for meteorological research. In charge of the operation was one of Allen Dulles's most trusted lieutenants, Richard Bissell.

Known to colleagues as 'the smartest man in Washington', Bissell had flown to Britain a few weeks before. Here he inspected and approved the Lakenheath base and personally won the per-mission of the Prime Minister, Eden, for the flights. In London the top secret operation was known as Aquatone. Dulles had already personally briefed the Foreign Secretary, Selwyn Lloyd, on the project in Washington. U-2 intelligence, he promised, would be fully shared with the British. But Eden was nervous. He had set considerable store on improving East–West relations and delayed permission until after the visit of Bulganin and Khrushchev. Then with the Buster Crabb affair he lost his nerve. Turning down a powerful plea by Selwyn Lloyd, Eden flatly forbade the operation from being based on British soil. Bissell and his CIA team promptly moved to Wiesbaden in Germany and began U-2 flights from there, as well as from bases in Turkey.

Eden resigned later that year following the Suez fiasco. His successor, Harold Macmillan, lifted the ban after meeting Eisenhower at their summit in Bermuda in March 1957. Here, too, the two leaders agreed that their intelligence experts should meet along with Canadian colleagues in Washington to establish an effective machinery for the rapid tripartite exchange of intelligence 'on any sudden threat of Soviet aggression against the Nato area'.[2]

The U-2 inaugurated a new era of technical intelligence geared at giving precise advance knowledge of Soviet preparations for attack. By 1959 Bissell even claimed that it was delivering 'ninety per cent of our hard intelligence about the Soviet Union'. Allen Dulles, true to form, boasted that he was able to get a look at 'every blade of grass in the Soviet Union'. The U-2 could capture licence plate numbers and, more important, by capturing images of Soviet bomber and missile bases, it convinced the West that Soviet claims of a massive arms build-up were mostly empty braggadocio on Khrushchev's part.[3]

Soon after that, satellite reconnaissance took over, rendering even the Lockheed plane redundant. Suddenly the glory days of clandestine cloak and dagger seemed over. Inside the CIA and SIS the tunnel quickly became a part of institutional history, a legend burnished by constant retelling into an almost mythical episode of Cold War glory and derring-do. The MI5 spycatcher maverick Peter Wright later claimed that SIS remained fixated on the tunnel. 'They were always looking for a successor,' he wrote, 'something on the epic scale which would have the Americans thirsting to share in the product. But they never found it.' By contrast, however, another intelligence insider remembered that very quickly even veterans of the tunnel were recalling it nostalgically as firmly ensconced in the good old days of the past.[4]

★

George Blake passed an anxious few weeks while the CIA and SIS investigated the reasons for the tunnel's discovery. Relieved by the result, he resumed his routine in Berlin. Then, in the summer of 1959 he was transferred back to London to work in the Soviet section of the Directorate of Production of SIS, based in Artillery Mansions, a large redbrick block of flats on Victoria Street ten minutes' walk from the SIS head office. Here, under his boss Dicky Franks – later a head of the service – he busily set about meeting people in the private sector: businessmen, university dons, students, artists, scientists and journalists – anyone who had regular contacts with Soviet citizens and could be cultivated as a long-term source of information. A year later he was sent to study Arabic at the Middle East Centre for Arabic Studies in Lebanon. In both London and Beirut he reported regularly to his KGB control.

But by now the net was closing in. While Blake was still in Berlin the CIA office there received a mysterious approach volunteering high-grade intelligence about the Soviets. David Murphy, who by now had taken over the Berlin base from Bill Harvey, carefully cultivated the source, whom he code-named 'Sniper'. The information arrived by letter written in German, but it revealed considerable knowledge of Polish and KGB operations. Some of it, although obscure, was sensational, not least the hint that the KGB was running a high-level spy in SIS. 'Sniper' code-named this source 'Lambda 2'.

In London a CIA officer passed on the lead to MI5 and SIS, who began an urgent internal inquiry. Several SIS officers had had access to the reports that 'Sniper' claimed to have seen. One of them was Blake. Although he was temporarily exonerated, investigations continued. Then, in January 1961, 'Sniper' physically defected to Murphy's base in Berlin and identified himself as Lieutenant-Colonel Michael Goleniewski, a former deputy head of Polish counter-intelligence. His debriefings, combined with the continuing queries inside SIS, pointed decisively to Blake as 'Lambda 2'.

Summoned back to London, Blake reported to the personnel department in Petty France. Here he was greeted by Harry Shergold, an old friend and Broadway's expert on Soviet affairs.

'How about a stroll across the park?' suggested Shergold. About twenty minutes later Blake found himself crossing the Mall, mounting the Duke of York steps, and back in the familiar lush surroundings of 2 Carlton Gardens. Shergold was skilful, and after three days Blake confessed. Before being formally arrested by Special Branch officers he was taken off to spend a weekend at Shergold's country cottage in Hampshire. 'We went for walks, only there was a Special Branch officer behind us', recalled Blake later in Moscow, 'I remember I made pancakes. I was really rather good at that.'[5]

From Broadway Sir Dick White, Sinclair's successor as head of the service, sent an urgent personal telegram to Peter Lunn in Bonn. A high-level traitor had been unmasked and Lunn would

A picture of George Blake issued by Scotland Yard after his dramatic escape from Wormwood Scrubs prison

have to inform the West Germans, it said. The name, added White, would be sent in an immediately following message. Playing a wild guessing name about possible candidates, Lunn personally decrypted the name. It was not what he expected. He had implicitly trusted Blake and was shattered by the news. It was April 1961, five years to the month since Stopwatch/Gold had been uncovered. To his interrogators in London, Blake had already confessed that he informed his KGB control about allied plans for the tunnel before he had left for Berlin.[6] Lunn now suddenly learned that his brainchild had been completely betrayed from the start. In May, Blake was tried in camera at the Old Bailey. Found guilty on all main charges, he was sentenced to forty-two years' imprisonment, said to be one year for every agent he had betrayed to Moscow.

★

Blake's treachery immediately altered perspectives on the tunnel. If Moscow had known about it from the start, then surely it could not have been the success so widely trumpeted by Allen Dulles and the CIA? It must, instead, have offered the KGB a perfect opportunity to use it for misinformation and deception. The intelligence was not gold or even silver, but fool's gold, false and worthless. Four years' planning and hard work, and millions of dollars, had been uselessly poured down the drain. The KGB once again had tricked the naïve Americans and penetrated the rotten SIS. The Cold War intelligence game was being played by fools, charlatans and rogues.

Such was the view of many critics. Blake's dramatic escape in 1966 from Wormwood Scrubs prison in London and his subsequent reappearance in Moscow only hardened this view of a skilful KGB outwitting a bumbling west. The former CIA agent Victor Marchetti, whose 'tell-all' book (with John D. Marks) *The CIA and the Cult of Intelligence* created a firestorm of controversy in the 1970s, claimed that even the real intelligence the tunnel garnered amounted to nothing more than 'tons of trivia and gossip'. A decade later the British journalist Chapman Pincher, author of several books claiming to expose the inadequacies and Soviet penetration of British intelligence, declared that 'the operation . . . produced nothing but a mass of carefully prepared misinformation, interspersed with occasional accurate "chicken-feed" to keep the operation going'. Yet another British-based journalist, Philip Knightley, whose iconoclastic treatment of the intelligence community *The Second Oldest Profession* enjoyed worldwide sales, denounced the entire operation as 'a fiasco' and a massive propaganda victory for the KGB. Tony Le Tissier, a former British commandant of Spandau prison, supported the view. 'The Soviets', he wrote, 'were able to set up their own special team to occupy and mislead western intelligence sources.' The American Mark Perry, author of the prematurely entitled *Eclipse: The Last Days of the CIA*, described Stopwatch/Gold as 'a stark defeat' because of its manipulation by the Soviets for dis-information. A retired KGB colonel, Oleg Nechiporenko, whose chief claim to fame was meeting Lee Harvey Oswald in Mexico City two months before President Kennedy's assassina-tion, pursued a similar line in his book *Passport to Assassination.*[7]

But the end of the Cold War, the collapse of the Soviet Union and a flood of revelations about KGB operations have produced a startling and unexpected twist to this interpretation. The most extraordinary consequence occurred in Berlin in 1999, ten years after the collapse of the wall. Here, at a round table conference planned jointly by ex-CIA and ex-KGB officers, a large group of practitioners and experts from both sides of the former Cold War divide sat down to exchange reminiscences and opinions about some of its most spectacular and controversial operations. The conference site itself spoke volumes about Berlin's pivotal place in the story. The Teufelsberg, or 'Devil's Mountain', more fre-quently known to insiders as 'The Hill', formed a complex of buildings in the British sector standing atop a huge mound of rubble built from the bombed-out debris of Hitler's capital. For years it had served as a hi-tech allied radar and electronic listen-ing post beamed over the wall behind the Iron Curtain. The end of the Cold War had made it redundant. But it was an ideal spot for a conference of ex-spooks. Many also seized the chance to visit other nearby landmarks. Hugh Montgomery, for one, particularly enjoyed his visit to the old Stasi headquarters. Vaulting the guard rope in the old office of the East German Minister of State Security, Erich Mielke, and spinning around in the desk chair, he chuckled 'It's nice to find it empty' before expertly flicking up the lid of the Stasi boss's old typewriter and giving the ribbon a quick once-over for latent images.[8]

The Teufelsberg meeting had been conceived six years before during a visit to Moscow in 1993 by David Murphy to make contact with his former Cold War opponents. It was Easter, and after enjoying Russian Orthodox ceremonies Murphy and George Bailey, a former director of Radio Liberty in Munich, were picked up at their hotel by the head of the public affairs bureau of the SVR (successor to the KGB). 'Well, Mr Murphy', boomed the Russian, 'how did you like spending the weekend in Moscow without surveillance?' One of Murphy's main missions was to contact Sergei Kondrashev, Blake's control in London and former head of the KGB's German division. Together with Bailey the three then agreed to co-operate in writing a book entitled *Battleground Berlin*, an extensive, gripping and groundbreaking account of the CIA v. KGB struggles during the decades-long Cold War battle over Berlin. Along with a set of previously classified CIA documents about Berlin handed out to every participant, it provided the essential background to the historic Teufelsberg events.

It was a doubly extraordinary occasion. Painfully noticeable by their absence were any participants from Britain's SIS. This was especially true of the fit and active Peter Lunn, still skiing regularly in Switzerland and the true originator of Stopwatch/ Gold. The agency had held firmly to its blanket rule that there should be no discussion or acknowledgment of its operations after 1945, even if this meant that credit for the Berlin tunnel fell entirely by default to the CIA and the Americans. Oleg Gordievsky, the KGB defector to Britain whose assessments of Mikhail Gorbachev's policy of *glasnost* had been so crucial to the

Thatcher government in the 1980s, took part in the Teufelsberg discussions. He made the obvious point. 'The impression was given', he noted angrily, 'that the intelligence war was fought and won by the Americans alone. It was very humiliating for Britain.'[9]

If the vital British role in Stopwatch/Gold remained concealed, the other evidence that was now placed on the table revealed an astonishing truth. The critics had been entirely wrong about the KGB response to Blake's treachery. Far from using the tunnel for misinformation and deception, the KGB's First Chief Directorate had taken a deliberate decision to conceal its existence from the Red Army and GRU, the main users of the cables being tapped. The reason for this extraordinary decision was to protect 'Diomid', their rare and brilliant source George Blake.

Blake's revelation about the tunnel had placed the KGB in an all too familiar 'Catch-22' situation. On the one hand, knowing that the West was listening in, they could use the cables to send misleading messages for some carefully calculated disinformation or deception campaign to fool their opponents. But if they did, they might be found out. It was not hard for Moscow to guess that the West might have other intelligence sources against which they could measure the accuracy of the intelligence being collected by the tunnel. If the West once guessed that a deception campaign was afoot, they would immediately realize that the Soviets knew about the tunnel. This would instantly spark a mole hunt, which would inevitably lead to George Blake, one of the small handful of their operatives to know about it. But Blake was still in place in the West, a jewel in their crown who might in the future lead them to even more glittering intelligence information. Did they dare risk him? On the other hand, if they did nothing, they would be allowing the West to listen in to real and untarnished secrets from the front line of the Cold War.

The pros and cons were carefully weighed within the First Chief Directorate of the KGB before Arseny Vasilievich

Tishkov, deputy chief of the directorate in charge of operational–technical matters, finally issued a directive to KGB departmental chiefs on 9 April 1954. Any disinformation operations designed to exploit the tunnel, he declared, had to be based on foolproof cover so as not to compromise the real source (Blake), and all proposals had to be submitted to him for approval. In other words, it was up to Tishkov to decide what, if anything, should be done to exploit the tunnel for disinformation purposes. But, as Kondrashev well knew, Tishkov would turn down any proposal that held out even the slightest risk of betraying Blake.

Thirty-nine years later Kondrashev finally revealed the secret to Murphy in Moscow. 'The communications lines being tapped', he assured the former CIA Soviet head, 'were not used for disinformation. To do so would have involved too many people and would have risked Blake's security.' An example of the care taken by the KGB to protect Blake is provided by the way it handled his information about the Vienna tunnel operations. Although he handed the ninety-page file over to the KGB as early as September 1953, it was not until a full year later that KGB Chairman Serov forwarded it to the Soviet Defence Minister; and by then SIS had actually terminated the operation. Obviously, to protect Blake, the KGB was ultimately ready to let the West listen in on the Red Army. Such bureaucratic rivalry, or turf wars, are not unusual. 'The picture of the KGB coolly sacrificing GRU and Soviet Army secrets to preserve its own mole', noted CIA historian Donald Steury at Teufelsberg, 'is one that resonates with Western perceptions and Soviet ruthlessness in military and intelligence matters.'[10]

Joe Evans, like David Murphy, was also keen to discuss the whole affair with his former Cold War opponents. Through an intermediary, he recorded later,

> Kondrashev categorically denied that a single item of disinformation or deception was ever disseminated through the Berlin tunnel. Not that the idea didn't occur to the

KGB, he added – suggestions were solicited from the few officers at the KGB center in Moscow who knew about the CIA–MI6 operation. All proposals were rejected as being too risky, i.e. too vulnerable to confirmation and detection, and too complicated; at best, the Center decided, disinformation could supply only small and questionable benefits of short-range impact.[11]

It would not be true, however, to say that the KGB did nothing. Kondrashev told Evans that twice the KGB issued a general warning to Marshal Grechko and the Red Army command in Germany to increase their telephone security. The alert was cast in vague and general terms so as not to suggest that the KGB actually knew the Red Army cables were being tapped; that would have dangerously extended knowledge of the operation even within the Soviet Union, and thus broadened the risk to Blake. But here lay the problem. A too specific alert was out of the question, but a general one, such as was actually issued, failed to set off any urgent alarms and was ignored. Joe Evans claimed on the basis of his own experience in analysing the conversations that Red Army generals were among the last people to obey instructions from anyone about how to behave on the telephone. NCOs attached to the KGB's Third Directorate, which supervised counter-intelligence and security in the Red Army, randomly tuned into conversations and would occasionally berate the speakers for violating telephone security. But, noted Evans, 'the higher the speaker's rank, the lower seemed a KGB non-com's nerve to dress him down.' The higher the rank, concluded Evans, the less secure the conversation.[12]

That the KGB had chosen to protect Blake at the expense of letting Stopwatch/Gold develop as a successful operation had been implicitly suggested early on by Allen Dulles himself in his book *The Craft of Intelligence*. It was published two years after Blake's trial, when he had described the tunnel as 'one of the most valuable and daring projects ever undertaken' by the CIA. Others had followed, mostly those with sources close to the CIA.

Among them were Harry Rositzke, a former Munich-based CIA officer who had run operations into the Soviet Union, David Martin, author of *Wilderness of Mirrors*, a best-seller about the controversial CIA counter-intelligence expert James Jesus Angleton, and John Ranelagh, author of *The Agency*.[13]

George Blake himself also confirmed the analysis. Ironically, of course, having first betrayed the tunnel, he had then became the inadvertent guardian of its integrity. Still living in Moscow at the time of the Teufelsberg discussions, he gave his own version of events in an interview for television. 'I was secretary at the meeting [of December 1953]', he confirmed,

> and so I was able to draw a very simple sketch which showed how the tunnel was going to run and what cables it was intended to attack. I was able to give [Kondrashev] this sketch . . . the next time we met he told me that he'd been to Moscow, that they were very impressed by this scheme as such, but that they were going to let it go on, in order to protect me, and that is what was done . . . I'm sure 99.9% of the information obtained by the SIS and CIA from the tunnel was genuine.[14]

Until and unless further evidence emerges it seems safe to conclude that Stopwatch/Gold was, as Allen Dulles and other Western sources so triumphantly proclaimed at the time, an outstanding and brilliant intelligence success.

Epilogue

By the late 1980s local memories of the tunnel had faded or disappeared, and the site itself had been transformed by the steady growth of Berlin. The ambience was best captured by the British novelist Ian McEwan, who reconnoitred the site for his 1987 novel *The Innocent*, which is based on Stopwatch/Gold. Thirty years after the tunnel's closure his protagonist, the callow young British post office technician Leonard Marnham, returns to the Rudow site. He finds that the refugee shacks and the allotment sheds so beloved by Berliners have been replaced by modern concrete flats. Suburban villas are springing up all around. The site of the 'radar station' is encircled by a double perimeter fence, but the buildings have been levelled and a sign proclaims that the site now belongs to a market garden company. To one side a thick wooden cross marks the spot where two young men had been shot while attempting to cross the wall. The only above-ground evidence that remains of the tunnel are a couple of wrecked sentry huts, some crumbling concrete floors with weeds bursting through and a large pit where the basement used to be.[1]

Six years later the American author Peter Grose, following the Allen Dulles trail for his biography of the CIA Director, also explored the site. By now everything, yet nothing, had changed. The wall had suddenly collapsed, as had the German Democratic

The long-abandoned tunnel is rediscovered in 1997 as redevelopment of the reunited city proceeds apace

Tunnel section exposed to the light after lying forgotten for four decades under the soil of Berlin

Republic, the Soviet Union and even the KGB itself. But in Rudow and Alt-Glienicke the passage of time itself was still obliterating the past. A local amateur historian showed Grose around. They crossed the line where the hated wall had once stood, and walked along the Schönefelder Chaussee. A super new highway had been constructed to Schönefeld Airport and the Chaussee, now bypassed, was being repaired as a pleasant and quiet residential street. 'His daughter laughed as we climbed through little garden plots', recorded Grose, 'saying "There is not a single other person in this village who could have told you about all this old stuff".'[2]

One person who could, however, was already on the trail. Soon afterwards a photographer was prowling around Rudow. His name was Willie Durie, a Scotsman who had worked as a photographer for the British forces until their withdrawal from the city. Now, as a freelancer, he was making a visual record of the allied Cold War presence in Berlin before massive post-unification rebuilding in the new German capital obliterated its remnants. Armed with his camera, Durie was exploring Rudow, where bulldozers were clearing the ground for construction work, looking for evidence of the tunnel. So in 1997, when a mechanical digger unexpectedly unearthed a section of metallic tube from the sandy earth, Durie knew instantly what it was. Strenuous and successful efforts followed, led by Helmut Trotnow, Director of the Allied Museum in Berlin, to save at least one section of the physical remnants of Stopwatch/Gold for history. When David Murphy and his co-authors launched their book, they were able to hold a press conference at the site. 'After 41 years', headlined the *Berliner Zeitung* beside a photograph showing Murphy and Kondrashev crouching in front of a salvaged section of tunnel, 'the former CIA chief and his KGB colleague meet again in an historic spot.'[3] By the time of the Teufelsberg conference, a 15 metre length, including its lining of sandbags and intricate spider's web of piping and wires, was fully restored to form the centrepiece and highlight of the Allied Museum.

This, now, is all that physically remains of Stopwatch/Gold. Yet even after the end of the Cold War it has retained some potency. Before former President George Bush visited the museum to inspect the tunnel in 1999, FBI sniffer dogs went wild. Fearing a bomb, secret service men desperately searched the tunnel. What they uncovered would undoubtedly have warmed the heart of Bill Harvey. Still clinging to the steel tubing were residues of the explosive his team had planted to stop a Soviet incursion.

What was the importance of the tunnel? Even those who reject the the theory of its use for deception are sometimes dubious. 'Intelligence analysts on the receiving end were underwhelmed with the fruits of all [the] labour', writes one recent historian of the CIA quoting a comment by Gordon Stewart, a former chief of the agency's foreign intelligence staff. Allen Dulles kept asking 'Is there anything interesting?', recalled Stewart, 'but there never was.'[4]

But if the principal reason for listening in was to warn of impending attack, 'nothing interesting' was precisely what Washington and London hoped to hear. In the years so dominated by nightmares of nuclear attack, no news was good news. Britain's Room 40 in the First World War, its naval and diplomatic code-breaking centre, had likewise revealed negative and profoundly reassuring indications about the plans of the Kaiser's high seas fleet as they recorded how infrequently it left port. A generation later its successor, Bletchley Park, had likewise provided gratifyingly negative indicators about Hitler's invasion plans. Secure in this knowledge, allied leaders had been able to plan ahead.

But could similar conclusions have been reached without the massive expense of the tunnel? Above ground, after all, Brixmis and other allied missions were roving through East Germany looking for any signs of Red Army preparations for invasion, and what they could see with their own eyes often appeared to tell them that Moscow was clearly neither prepared nor able to mount an attack on the West. Yet intelligence analysts are professional pessimists, always prepared for the worst-case scenario

– and in the 1950s still deeply scarred by recent history. Had anyone actually seen the Japanese carrier fleet taking its deadly cargo of aircraft towards Pearl Harbor, they might have asked. Would the Soviets really be so foolish as to scatter visible evidence around if they were planning an attack? Obviously not, thought Western intelligence analysts. If further proof were needed of their ingrained caution, it is provided by Britain's Joint Intelligence Committee in March 1956, only a month before the Soviets 'discovered' the tunnel and while the West was still digesting the contents of Khrushchev's remarkable secret speech. 'So long as the Soviets have the initiative', declared the British intelligence chiefs, 'any attack will be carefully planned and prepared. We believe that they will rate the importance of achieving strategic surprise with their initial nuclear strikes so highly that they will not allow any detectable preparation or movement of their ground forces that would jeopardise such surprise.' But, they noted ominously, 'The Group of Soviet Forces in Germany is, however, offensive in pattern and could launch a limited offensive without previous build up.' In short, the listeners in of Stopwatch/Gold were needed as much now as ever before.[5]

It also became quickly apparent that, quite apart from its strategic importance, the tunnel promised rich rewards in other fields. The Kremlin was still largely a closed book to the West. Stalin might be dead, but what were his successsors up to? What plans did they have for Germany and Europe? And who was really running the show anyway? Western intelligence services were largely in the dark about the answers but under strong and persistent pressure from their political masters to produce. And if they looked to their spymasters for results, they in turn needed weapons to protect themselves and their agencies from the opponent. All the better, therefore, if the Berlin tunnel could reveal important inside information about KGB or GRU operations directed against the CIA and SIS.

One other way of evaluating the tunnel has also been suggested. Given that the KGB knew about it, perhaps there was another reason (besides that of protecting Blake) for their failure

to use it for deception. Perhaps, suggests Peter Grose in his biography of Allen Dulles, the KGB was secretly acting in the inter-
ests of *détente*. Knowing that no attack on the West was planned,
they wanted London and Washington to know that. And so, he
postulates, they were quite happy not to confuse the listeners-in
but to let them hear what was really going on.[6] On the surface
it is an intriguing idea – except that none of those on the Soviet
side who have spoken about the tunnel has ever bothered to
make the claim, which they surely would have done after the end
of the Cold War made it possible for them to don the mantle of
saviours of peace.

Notes

ACKNOWLEDGEMENTS

1. D. E. Murphy, S. A. Kondrashev and G. Bailey, *Battleground Berlin: CIA vs. KGB in the Cold War.*

INTRODUCTION

1. P. Lewis, *The Fifties*, p. 98.
2. *The Times* (6 March 2001); see also issues for 5 and 12 March, and *Daily Telegraph* (5, 12 March 2001).
3. R. Aldrich, *The Hidden Hand: Britain, America, and Cold War Secret Intelligence.*

1. 'THE STUFF OF WHICH THRILLER FILMS ARE MADE'

1. Quoted in A. Richie, *Faust's Metropolis*, p. 689.
2. I. Fleming, *Thrilling Cities*, p. 144.
3. Murphy, Kondrashev and Bailey, pp. 8, 256.
4. M. Wolf, *Memoirs of a Spymaster*, p. 90.
5. P. Grose, *Gentleman Spy*, p. 399.

2. OUR MAN IN VIENNA

1. C. Andrew and V. Mitrokhin, *The Mitrokhin File*, pp. 442–3; the KGB description of Lunn's tradecraft dates from his days as SIS chief in Beirut in the early 1960s.
2. D. Hart-Davis, *Hitler's Olympics*, p. 103.
3. *Who's Who* (1997), p. 1208; P. Lunn, *Evil in High Places*, p. 252; P. Lunn, *High-Speed Skiing*, pp. 125–6; P. Lunn, *Going Skiing*, p. 10.
4. S. Fesq, quoted in S. Dorril, *MI6*, p. 120; and W. Hood, *Mole*, p. 31.

5. W. B. Bader, *Austria between East and West, 1945–1955*, pp. 1–175.
6. G. Greene, *The Third Man*, pp. 13, 119; N. Sherry, *The Life of Graham Greene*, vol. 2, pp. 243–50.
7. G. Greene, *Ways of Escape*, p. 126; Sherry, p. 250.
8. P. S. Deriabin, with J. C. Evans, *Inside Stalin's Kremlin*, p. 200; Hood, p. 74.
9. G. Blake, *No Other Choice*, p. 8.
10. R. Steers, *FSS: Field Security Section*, p. ii.
11. For an illuminating sample of Field Security operations at this time, see Steers, especially pp. 58–9, 74–5, and 157–62. See also A. Clayton, *Forearmed: A History of the Intelligence Corps*, pp. 201–2.
12. D. Colley, 'Shadow Warriors', *VFW (Veterans of Foreign Wars)* (September 1997).
13. For Korda, the Z network and King's early SIS career, see A. Read and D. Fisher, *Colonel Z*, pp. 176–91, 230–31.
14. A. Cavendish, *Inside Intelligence: The Revelations of an MI6 Officer*, p. 75; and private information.
15. T. Bower, *The Perfect English Spy: Sir Dick White and the Secret War, 1935–1990*, p. 180.
16. Blake, p. 10.
17. Letter to the author from the SOE adviser at the Foreign and Commonwealth Office, dated 14 May 2001; and private information.
18. P. Wright, *Spycatcher*, p. 156; Bower, p. 348.
19. Wright, pp. 18–20, 47.

3. SMOKY JOE'S

1. Bob Steers, correspondence with the author.
2. M. Smith, *New Cloak, Old Dagger*, p. 116.
3. Blake, p. 9.
4. Cavendish, pp. 73–4.
5. Hood, pp. 28, 30–31.
6. D. Martin, *Wilderness of Mirrors*, pp. 74–5; J. Ranelagh, *The Agency: The Rise and Decline of the CIA*, pp. 138–9.
7. Martin, p. 76.
8. Ibid.; Ranelagh, p. 140; N. West, *Seven Spies Who Changed the World*, p. 139.
9. Bower, pp. 135–6.
10. David E. Murphy, letter to the author, 10 February 2000.

4. BLACK FRIDAY

1. S. Ambrose, *Ike's Spies: Eisenhower and the Intelligence Establishment*, p. 169.

2. M. Wolf, interview for *Cold War* television series, Jeremy Isaacs Productions.
3. Cavendish, p. 6.
4. Wright, p. 7.
5. Aldrich, pp. 10–11.
6. See, for example, J. E. Haynes and H. Kehr, *Venona: Decoding Soviet Espionage in America*; A. Weinstein and A. Vassiliev, *The Haunted Wood: Soviet Espionage in America: The Stalin Years*; N. West, *Venona: The Greatest Secret of the Cold War*; and R. L. Benson and M. Warner, *Venona: Soviet Espionage and the American Response*.
7. Bower, p. 144.
8. Donald Steury, commentary on his paper on the Berlin tunnel presented at the Berlin Conference 1998.
9. D. A. Hatch and R. L. Benson, *NSA Korean War 1950–1953 Commemoration: The Sigint Background*, p. 5.
10. C. Andrew, *For The President's Eyes Only: Secret Intelligence and the American Presidency from Washington to Bush*, p. 185.
11. Cited in Haynes and Kehr, *Venona*, p. 49.
12. KGB Archives, Moscow, File 43173, vol. 2v, 25–27; quoted in Weinstein and Vassiliev, pp. 291–2.
13. Hatch and Benson, p. 6. I am grateful to Matthew M. Aid for drawing this material to my attention.
14. Andrew, p. 197.

5. THE HUMAN FACTOR

1. R. Lewin, *The American Magic*, pp. 232–46.
2. Rowlett died in 1998. For appreciations see the *Daily Telegraph* (18 July 1998), *The Times* (15 July 1998) and F. B. Saxon, 'Wizard in Making and Breaking Codes', *New York Times* (2 July 1998). See also J. Bamford, *The Puzzle Palace*, pp. 152–6, 374. I am grateful to David Kahn for further information about Rowlett.
3. Martin, p. 68; R. Lamphere and T. Schachtman, *The FBI–KGB War*, p. 61; R. Powers, *The Man Who Kept Secrets*, p. 137; B. Hersh, *The Old Boys*, p. 187; E. Thomas, *The Very Best Men*, pp. 130–31.
4. S. Hersh, *The Dark Side of Camelot*, pp. 186–7.
5. O'Brien, interview with the author, Washington DC, April 2001.
6. 'The longest continuous sample . . .', see CIA Clandestine Services History: 'The Berlin Tunnel Operation, 1952–1956', CS Historical Paper 150, prepared 25 August 1967, published 24 June 1968. Declassified in 1977 and obtained by the author under FOIA request, 30 December 1999, ref. F-2000–00117. See also CIA: 'Field Project Outline, 16 September 1953', in *Documents on the*

Intelligence War in Berlin, 1946 to 1961, ed. D. Steury, pp. 442–6; and Murphy, Kondrashev and Bailey, pp. 209–12.

7. 'Fleetfoot', rather than 'Fleetwood', is, *pace* Murphy, the correct nickname of Harvey's linkman on the tunnel in Frankfurt. For Truscott, see Hersh, p. 409, and Thomas, p. 65.

6. 2 CARLTON GARDENS

1. M. Gilbert, *Winston S. Churchill*, vol. 8, p. 690; N. Rose, *Churchill: An Unruly Life*, p. 336.
2. Churchill to Minister of Defence, 30 July 1952, 'Personal and Secret', PRO, DEFE 13/352.
3. 'Likelihood of Total War with the Soviet Union to the end of 1954', memorandum from the Chiefs of Staff to the Minister of Defence, 28 May 1952, COS (52), 28 May 1952; and Minister of Defence to the Prime Minister, 3 August 1952, PRO, DEFE 13/352.
4. A. W. Buzzard, Director of Naval Intelligence, 'Summary of N.I.D.G.C. report no. 42 (Not to Nato)', March 1953, PRO, DEFE 13/352.
5. N. W. Brownjohn to the Minister of Defence, 26 June 1953, commenting on JIC (53), 11, 14, 36, 37, 38 and 39, PRO, DEFE 13/352.
6. D. Stafford, *Churchill and Secret Service*, p. 379.
7. P. Lashmar, *Spy Flights of the Cold War*, pp. 61–75.
8. Aldrich, p. 405.
9. Bower, p. 180.
10. Blake, pp. 11–14.

7. AGENT 'DIOMID'

1. Bower, p. 261.
2. Blake, p. 164; for Blake in general, see H. M. Hyde, *George Blake: Superspy*.
3. Blake, p. 160; for Rodin, see C. Andrew and O. Gordievsky, *KGB: The Inside Story*, pp. 322, 362–3; see also Andrew and Mitrokhin, p. 520.
4. *Sunday Times* (14 November 1999).
5. Murphy, Kondrashev and Bailey, p. 215; see also Kondrashev, as quoted in the *Sunday Times* (14 November 1999).
6. Murphy, Kondrashev and Bailey, pp. 36, 482–3; Blake, pp. 16–17.

8. OPERATION STOPWATCH/GOLD

1. Author's interview with Hugh Montgomery, Washington DC, April 2001.

2. Murphy, Kondrashev and Bailey, p. 213.
3. Thomas, p. 79.
4. See Ambrose, *Ike's Spies*, p. 714, and N. Miller, *Spying for America: The Hidden History of U.S. Intelligence*, p. 381. For Auchinloss, see Thomas, p. 73.
5. Quoted in Andrew, p. 202.
6. CIA History, *The Berlin Tunnel Operation, 1952–6*, pp. 6–10.
7. See A. Geraghty, *Beyond the Frontline: The Untold Exploits of Britain's Most Daring Cold War Spy Mission*, pp. 3, 35, 63. See also N. N. Wylde, ed., *The Story of Brixmis, 1946–90*, passim.

9. 'KILTS UP, BILL!'

1. A. Horne, *Back Into Power*, pp. 257–72.
2. Churchill to Field Marshal Alexander of Tunis, Minister of Defence, personal minute, 8 February 1954; G. L. McDermott, Foreign Office, to W. H. Hanna, Ministry of Defence, 9 February 1954; and Alexander to Churchill, 10 February 1954, PRO, DEFE 13/352.
3. 'Direction of Intelligence Effort' (Joint Services Intelligence Group [Germany] aide-memoire), JSIG(G)P(54)30, 19 July 1954, PRO, DEFE 14/90.
4. Aldrich, p. 327.
5. Ibid, p. 328.
6. Blake, p. 168.
7. Record of SIS/CIA meetings on Stopwatch/Gold held in London 15–18 December 1953, reproduced as Appendix 9 in Murphy, Kondrashev and Bailey, pp. 449–53. From files of the SVRA (the Foreign Intelligence Service of the Russian Federation).
8. Murphy, Kondrashev and Bailey, p. 217.
9. Note on 'Diomid' file, 12 February 1954, SVRA, Moscow; quoted in Murphy, Kondrashev and Bailey, p. 216.

10. DIGGING GOLD

1. Murphy p. 424; Grose, p. 407.
2. Martin, p. 81.
3. S. Ambrose, *Eisenhower*, vol. 2, pp. 226–8; Ranelagh, pp. 276–9; Andrew, p. 221; Grose, p. 346.
4. Ambrose, *Ike's Spies*, p. 188; R. Jeffreys-Jones, *The CIA and American Democracy*, pp. 74–5.
5. JIC (54) 82, 21 October 1954, PRO, CAB 158/18.
6. Martin, p. 83.

7. Murphy, Kondrashev and Bailey, p. 220; and interview with Hugh Montgomery, Washington DC, April 2001.
8. Details of the tunnel's construction are provided in the CIA internal history, in W. K. Harvey's progress report to General Truscott in Frankfurt of 18 October 1954, in D. Steury, pp. 338–44, and in Murphy, Kondrashev and Bailey, pp. 219–25.
9. JIC (55) 22nd, 10 March 1955, PRO, CAB 159/18.
10. 'Memorandum for the Record', dated 29 November 1954, a résumé of decisions reached on 18 November 1954. Steury, pp. 346–9.

11. TURNING ON THE TAP

1. Blake, p. 166.
2. Ibid., p. 174; Hyde, p. 46.
3. M. Beschloss, *Mayday: Eisenhower, Khrushchev and the U-2 Affair*, p. 103.
4. Ranelagh, p. 294.
5. See CIA History of the Berlin tunnel, section V, pp. 25–6, released in 1995; see also Murphy, Kondrashev and Bailey, p. 222.
6. Murphy, Kondrashev and Bailey, appendix 5, p. 423.

12. CHESTER TERRACE

1. Bower, p. 182.
2. J. C. Evans, 'Berlin Tunnel Intelligence: A Bumbling KGB', *International Journal of Intelligence and Counter-Intelligence*, vol. 9, no. 1 (1996), p. 43. For additional information on the Main Processing Unit in London I am deeply indebted to an interview with Joe Evans in April 2001.
3. Interview with the author, Florida, March 2001. For the Berlin base's 'Target Room', see Murphy, Kondrashev and Bailey, pp. 256–7.
4. For Popov and the Berlin base, see Murphy, Kondrashev and Bailey, pp. 267–70.

13. 'A BONANZA'

1. Evans, p. 47; and interview with the author, April–June 2001.
2. D. Holloway, *Stalin and the Bomb*, pp. 112, 177; W. Stiller with J. Adams, *Beyond the Wall: Memoirs of an East and West German Spy*, p. 171.
3. P. Maddrell, 'British–American Scientific Intelligence Collaboration during the Occupation of Germany', *American–British–Canadian*

Intelligence Relations, 1939–2000, ed. D. Stafford and R. Jeffreys-Jones, pp. 74–94.

4. Ibid., pp. 85–6; see also Murphy, Kondrashev and Bailey, pp. 13–15, 425, appendix 5.
5. Murphy, Kondrashev and Bailey, p. 425, appendix 5.
6. Evans, p. 46.
7. Murphy, Kondrashev and Bailey, p. 427.
8. Murphy, Kondrashev and Bailey, p. 427, appendix 5. Appendix B of the declassified CIA history of the tunnel entitled 'Recapitulation of the Intelligence Derived' has had all this material blanked out.

14. FINGERS CROSSED

1. Hood, pp. 72–3.
2. Murphy, Kondrashev and Bailey, pp. 44–6, 178.
3. It can be found in Steury, pp. 267–72.
4. Murphy, Kondrashev and Bailey, pp. 226.
5. 'Memorandum of Discussion at the 256th Meeting of the National Security Council', Washington DC, 10 November 1955, in *Foreign Relations of the United States 1955–1957*, vol. 26, *Central and Eastern Europe* (Washington DC, 1992), p. 399; See also National Intelligence Estimate (NIE) 'Probable Short-term Communist Capabilities and Intentions Regarding Berlin', number 11–3–56, 28 February 1956, in *Foreign Relations of the United States*, vol. 26, pp. 414–23. In the same volume (pp. 423–30), the National Security Council Report 5404/1, 'Progress Report on United States Policy Towards Berlin', dated 17 May 1956, covering events in Berlin from September 1955 to May 1956, contains no reference to the spy tunnel. It should be noted, however, that paragraph 14 in the list of major developments has not been declassified. For discussions on the dissolution of the Cominform, see *Foreign Relations of the United States 1955–57*, vol. 24, *Soviet Union and Eastern Mediterranean* (Washington DC, 1989), pp. 95–6. *Khrushchev Remembers*, introduced with a commentary by Edward Crankshaw (London Book Club Associates, 1971) contains no reference at all to the tunnel.
6. A. Dulles, *The Craft of Intelligence*, p. 202.
7. Joseph C. Evans, communication with the author.
8. Steury, p. 352.

15. 'IT'S GONE, JOHN'

1. Dulles, p. 202.

2. For the above details, see 'Discovery by the Soviets of the Tunnel', Appendix A to the CIA history of the Berlin tunnel, in Steury, pp. 351–65; Murphy, Kondrashev and Bailey, pp. 227–31. A section of the transcript recording conversations picked up by the microphone in the tap chamber is also to be found in Steury, pp. 367–93.

16. CAUGHT RED-HANDED

1. Hersh, p. 379.
2. Thomas, p. 129. For Barnes, see especially pp. 75–86.
3. Quoted in H. Zolling, 'The Affair of the CIA Tunnel', Appendix B in H. Hohne, *Network*, p. 306.
4. C. P. Hope, Bonn, to M. S. Williams, Foreign Office, 28 April 1956, in FO 371/124647.
5. NBC broadcast, 17 May 1956, in CIA history of the tunnel.
6. R. Gehlen, *The Gehlen Memoirs*, pp. 188–9.
7. Murphy, Kondrashev and Bailey, p. 206; Gehlen; E. H. Cookridge, *Gehlen: Spy of the Century*, pp. 282–6; Miller, p. 377; and Grose, pp. 397–8.
8. Cookridge, p. 282.
9. Murphy, Kondrashev and Bailey, p. 233. see Cookridge, p. 282, as an example of this myth.
10. Andrew and Mitrokhin, p. 522; see also Andrew and Gordievsky, p. 437.
11. *The Times* (25 April 1956).
12. Lewis, p. 108.
13. Murphy, Kondrashev and Bailey, p. 232.
14. See *Keesing's Contemporary Archives* (28 April to 5 May 1956), 14836–7.
15. For the Crabb affair, see N. West, *The Friends*, pp. 109–18, and Dorril, pp. 617–20.

17. 'A GANGSTER ACT'

1. Hersh, p. 379. See also Jeffreys-Jones, p. 107.
2. Beschloss, p. 117.
3. For East German press coverage, see the CIA history, Appendix D.
4. Hyde, p. 47.
5. C. P. Hope, Bonn, to M. S. Williams, Foreign Office, London, 28 April 1956, in PRO, FO 371/124647; and 'Review of Events in Berlin and the Soviet Zone, no. 18, for the Week Ending May 2, 1956' in Berlin to Bonn no. 33 of 2 May 1956, repeated to the Foreign Office in PRO, FO 371/1224356. Also Political Adviser, Berlin, to Chancellery, Bonn, 2 May 1956, loc. cit.

6. Report from Political Branch, British Military Government, Berlin, to Chancellery, Bonn, 8 May 1956, in PRO, FO 371/124647.

7. Report from Political Branch, British Military Government, Berlin, to Chancellery, Bonn, 9 May 1956, in PRO, FO 371/124647.

8. Blake, p. 181.

9. Martin, pp. 90–91, refers to Bronze, but sees it as a purely American idea.

18. TUNNEL VISIONS

1. CIA history of the tunnel, Appendix A, 'Discovery by the Soviets of the tunnel', 15 August 1956, in Steury, p. 351; author's interview with Hugh Montgomery, Washington DC, April 2001.

2. For Aquatone (later re-named Chess), see Selwyn Lloyd to Anthony Eden, PM/56/36 of 24 February 1956, and Lloyd to Eden of 14 May 1956, PM/56/91, plus related correspondence in PRO, AIR 19/826. See also Macmillan to Eisenhower, 22 March 1957, quoted in Aldrich, p. 102; Lashmar, p. 140; and R. Bissell, *Reflections of a Cold Warrior*, p. 115.

3. Beschloss, p. 5.

4. Wright, p. 72; private information.

5. Bower, pp. 255–70; Wright, p. 128; Murphy, Kondrashev and Bailey, pp. 343–8; Blake, pp. 181–205; and interview by George Blake for *Cold War* television series, Jeremy Isaacs Productions, roll 10975, 34.

6. CIA history of the tunnel, undated, Appendix G, in Steury, p. 395.

7. Marchetti and Marks, *The CIA and the Cult of Intelligence*, p. 9; C. Pincher, *Too Secret Too Long*; P. Knightley, *The Second Oldest Profession*, p. 291; M. Perry, *Eclipse: The Last Days of the CIA*; Murphy, Kondrashev and Bailey, p. 207; Evans, p. 43.

8. C. P. Wallace, 'Lies, Spies and Memories', *Time* (27 September 1999).

9. Letter to *Daily Telegraph* (15 September 1999).

10. Murphy, Kondrashev and Bailey, pp. 218–9.

11. Ibid., p. 218; Evans, p. 48.

12. Evans, p. 50.

13. Dulles, p. 202; Rositzke, *CIA's Secret Operations*, p. 146; Martin, p. 89; Ranelagh, pp. 288–96.

14. George Blake, interview for *Cold War* television series, roll 10976, 25.

Notes

EPILOGUE

1. I. McEwan, *The Innocent*, pp. 235–6. The novel (subtitled 'The Special Relationship') was transformed into a film of the same name, directed by John Schlesinger and starring Anthony Hopkins and Isabella Rossellini. I am grateful to Ian McEwan for providing some background details.
2. Grose, p. 399.
3. *Berliner Zeitung* (23 September 1997); see also 'Operation Gold', *Der Spiegel*, no. 39 (1997).
4. Thomas, pp. 128–9; see also Miller, p. 379.
5. Joint Intelligence Committee, 'Employment of the Soviet Armed Forces in the Land Campaign in the Event of Global War, 1956–1960', JIC (56) 5/Final, 2 March 1956, p. 4, CAB 158/23.
6. Grose, p. 401.

Bibliography

R. Aldrich, *The Hidden Hand: Britain, America and Cold War Secret Intelligence*, London, John Murray, 2001

S. Ambrose, *Eisenhower*, vol. 2, *The Presidency*, New York, Simon and Schuster, 1984

—, *Ike's Spies*, New York, Doubleday, 1981

C. Andrew, *For the President's Eyes Only: Secret Intelligence and the American Presidency from Washington to Bush*, London, Harper Collins, 1996

C. Andrew and O. Gordievsky, *KGB: The Inside Story*, London, Hodder and Stoughton, 1990

C. Andrew and V. Mitrokhin, *The Mitrokhin File*, London, Penguin, 2000

W. B. Bader, *Austria between East and West 1945–1955*, Stanford, Stanford University Press, 1966

J. Bamford, *The Puzzle Palace*, London, Sidgwick and Jackson, 1983

R. L. Benson and M. Warner, *Venona: Soviet Espionage and the American Response*, Washington DC, NSA/CIA, 1996

M. Beschloss, *Mayday: Eisenhower, Khrushchev and the U-2 Affair*, London, Faber and Faber, 1986

R. Bissell, *Reflections of a Cold Warrior*, New Haven, Yale University Press, 1996

G. Blake, *No Other Choice*, London, Cape, 1990

T. Bower, *The Perfect English Spy: Sir Dick White and the Secret War, 1935–1990*, London, Heinemann, 1995

A. Cavendish, *Inside Intelligence: The Revelations of an MI6 Officer*, London, HarperCollins, 1997

A. Clayton, *Forearmed: A History of the Intelligence Corps*, London, Brassey's, 1993

Bibliography

E. H. Cookridge, *George Blake: Double Agent*, New York, Ballantine, 1970

—, *Gehlen: Spy of the Century*, London, Hodder and Stoughton, 1971

P. H. J. Davies, *The British Secret Services*, Oxford, ABC Clio, 1996

—, 'Organisational Development of Britain's Secret Intelligence Service 1909–1979', PhD thesis, University of Reading, 1997

P. Deriabin, with J. C. Evans, *Inside Stalin's Kremlin*, Dulles, VA, Brassey's, 1998

S. Dorril, *MI6: Fifty Years of Special Operations*, London, Fourth Estate, 2000

A. Dulles, *The Craft of Intelligence*, London, Weidenfeld and Nicolson, 1963

N. Elliott, *Never Judge a Man by His Umbrella*, Salisbury, M. Russell, 1991

J. C. Evans, 'Berlin Tunnel Intelligence: A Bumbling KGB', *International Journal of Intelligence and Counter-Intelligence*, 9/1 (Spring 1996)

I. Fleming, *Thrilling Cities*, London, Cape, 1963

R. Gehlen, *The Gehlen Memoirs*, London, Collins, 1972

A. Geraghty, *Beyond the Frontline: The Untold Exploits of Britain's Most Daring Cold War Spy Mission*, London, HarperCollins, 1996

M. Gilbert, *Winston S. Churchill*, vol. 8, London, Minerva, 1990

G. Greene, *The Third Man*, London, Penguin, 1971

—, *Ways of Escape*, London, The Bodley Head, 1980

A. Grose, *Gentleman Spy: The Life of Allen Dulles*, London, André Deutsch, 1995

D. Hart-Davis, *Hitler's Olympics*, London, Coronet, 1988

D. A. Hatch and R. L. Benson, *NSA Korean War, 1950–53, Commemoration: The Sigint Background*, Washington DC, NSA, 2000

J. E. Haynes and H. Kehr, *Venona: Decoding Soviet Espionage in America*, New Haven and London, Yale University Press, 2000

P. Hennessy, 'The Itch after the Amputation? The Purposes of British Intelligence as the Century Turns: An Historical Perspective and Forward Look', *War, Resistance and Intelligence: Essays in Honour of M.R.D. Foot*, ed. K. G. Robertson, Barnsley, Leo Cooper, 1999

B. Hersh, *The Old Boys: The American Elite and the Origins of the CIA*, New York, Scribners, 1992

H. Hohne, *The General Was a Spy*, London, Pan, 1973

D. Holloway, *Stalin and the Bomb*, London, Yale University Press, 1994

W. Hood, *Mole*, London, Weidenfeld and Nicolson, 1982

A. Horne, *Back into Power*, London, Max Parrish, 1955

T. Huntington, 'The Berlin Spy Tunnel Affair', *American Heritage of Invention and Technology*, 10/4 (Spring 1995)

Bibliography

H. M. Hyde, *George Blake, Superspy*, London, Futura, 1988

R. Jeffreys-Jones, *The CIA and American Democracy*, New Haven, Yale University Press, 1998

O. Kalugin, *Spymaster*, London, Smith Gryphon, 1994

P. Knightley, *The Second Oldest Profession*, London, André Deutsch, 1986

R. Lamphere and T. Schachtman, *The FBI–KGB War*, London, W.H. Allen, 1988

P. Lashmar, *Spy Flights of the Cold War*, Sutton, 1996

W. Leary, 'The Berlin Tunnel: Success or Failure?', unpublished paper delivered at the Akademie für Politische Bildung, Tutzing, Germany, June 1999

A. Le Tissier, *Berlin Then and Now*, London, Battle of Britain Prints, 1992

R. Lewin, *The American Magic*, London, Penguin, 1983

P. Lewis, *The Fifties*, London, Heinemann, 1978

P. Lunn, *Evil in High Places*, London, Methuen, 1947

—, *High-Speed Skiing*, London, Methuen, 1935

V. Marchetti and J. D. Marks, *The CIA and the Cult of Intelligence*, Knopf, New York, 1974

D. C. Martin, *Wilderness of Mirrors*, New York, Ballantine, 1981

I. McEwan, *The Innocent*, London, Vintage, 1998

N. Miller, *Spying for America:The Hidden History of U.S. Intelligence,* New York, Dell, 1989

Y. Modin, *My Five Cambridge Friends*, London, Headline, 1994

D. E. Murphy, S. A. Kondrashev and G. Bailey, *Battleground Berlin: CIA vs KGB in the Cold War*, New Haven and London, Yale University Press, 1997

M. Perry, *The Last Days of the CIA*, New York, Morrow, 1992

C. Pincher, *Too Secret Too Long*, London, Sidgwick and Jackson, 1984

R. Powers, *The Man Who Kept the Secrets*, London, Weidenfeld and Nicolson, 1980

J. Ranelagh, *The Agency:The Rise and Decline of the CIA*, New York, Simon and Schuster, 1986

A. Read and D. Fisher, *Colonel Z*, London, Hodder and Stoughton, 1984

A. Richie, *Faust's Metropolis*, London, HarperCollins, 1998

N. Rose, *Churchill:An Unruly Life*, London, Simon and Schuster, 1995

H. Rositzke, *CIA's Secret Operations*, New York, Reader's Digest Press, 1977

N. Sherry, *The Life of Graham Greene*, vol. 2, London, Cape, 1994

M. Smith, *New Cloak, Old Dagger*, London, Gollancz, 1996

D. Stafford, *Churchill and Secret Service*, London, John Murray, 1997

D. Stafford and R. Jeffreys-Jones, eds., *American–British–Canadian Intelligence Relations 1939–2000*, London, Cass, 2000

R. Steers, *FSS:Field Security Section*, Sussex, Eastlays, 1996

D. P. Steury, ed., *Documents on the Intelligence War in Berlin 1946 to 1961*, Washington DC, CIA History Staff, Center for the Study of Intelligence, 1999

W. Stiller, with J. Adams, *Beyond the Wall: Memoirs of an East and West German Spy*, Washington, Brassey's, 1992

E. Thomas, *The Very Best Men*, New York, Simon and Schuster, 1995

C. P. Wallace, 'Lies, Spies and Memories', *Time* (27 September 1999)

A. Weinstein and A. Vassiliev, *The Haunted Wood: Soviet Espionage in America:The Stalin Era*, New York, Random House, 1999

N. West, *The Friends,* London, Coronet, 1990

—, *Seven Spies Who Changed the World*, London, Secker and Warburg, 1991

—, *Venona:The Greatest Secret of the Cold War*, London, HarperCollins, 1999

M. Wolf, *Memoirs of a Spymaster*, London, Pimlico, 1998

P. Wright, *Spycatcher*, Toronto, Stoddart, 1987

N. N. Wylde, ed., *The Story of Brixmis, 1946–1990*, Brixmis Association, n.p., n.d.

Picture Credits

The author and publishers would like to thank the following for permission to reproduce illustrations: p. 9, private collection; pp. 15 (below), 68, 161 and 176, © Hulton Archive; p. 62, Imperial War Museum, London; pp. 106, 108, 119, 168 and 185, W. Durie; p. 118 (above), US National Archives. Map on pp. 80–1 © W. Durie, 1997.

Index

Page numbers in *italic* indicate illustrations

Index

Blake, George (*cont.*)
  confesses to betrayal, 176–7; portrayed,
  176; escape from Wormwood Scrubs,
  177; KGB protects over secrecy of
  Berlin tunnel, 180–3, 188
Blake, Gillian (*née* Allan), 70, 114
Bletchley Park, 60, 65, 187
Bonn, 6
Brandt, Willy, 167
Britain: keeps tunnel involvement secret,
  12, 160–1, 163, 169, 179; Khrushchev
  and Bulganin visit, 12, 161–4; defectors
  and traitors, 39–40; code-breaking pact
  with USA (1948), 51, 61; discrepancy
  with USA on estimates of Soviet
  equipment, 110
Brixmis (British C in C's Mission to the
  Soviet Forces of Occupation in
  Germany), 85, 129, 187
Brown, George (*later* Baron George-
  Brown), 162
Brundrett, Freddie, 44, 48
Bulganin, Nikolai, 12, 115, 161–4, *161*, 173
Burgess, Guy, 39–40, 73
Bush, George (senior), 187

Caccia, Harold (*later* Baron), 24
Callahan, Joan, 47
Carlton Gardens (no. 2): as 'Y' Section
  HQ, 63, *64*, 65–6, 91
Castro, Fidel, 53
Cavendish, Anthony: in Vienna, 24, 34; in
  Germany, 43; *Inside Intelligence*, 24
Central Intelligence Agency (CIA):
  denounced by USSR after discovery of
  tunnel, 1, 157–8, 165–6; co-operates on
  Operation Stopwatch/Gold, 2–4, 182;
  activities in Berlin, 7, 56, 77;
  information on Vienna tunnel, 36–8;
  Office of Communications, 36; and
  warnings of Red Army attacks, 36;
  formed, 42; Office of Special
  Operations, 51, 53; Staff 'D', 63, 124;
  increased activities under Eisenhower,
  83; Joseph McCarthy attacks, 103; T-32
  division (for processing), 119–20; officers
  at Chester Terrace, 122, 124–6; and
  Soviet nuclear programme, 134; relations
  with President, 165
Chester Terrace, Regent's Park, London,
  122, *123*, 124–6, 127
Chesterton, G.K.: *The Hammer of God*, 17
China: Communist triumph in, 43; and
  exposure of Berlin tunnel, 157
Churchill, (Sir) Winston S.: and SOE, 26;

intelligence demands, 58–61, 87, 89–90,
  104; fears attack by USSR, 59, 89–90;
  and Bletchley Park, 60, 65; Bermuda
  summit with Eisenhower (1953), 88, 91,
  93; honours, 91; and relations with
  USA, 93
Ciano, Countess Galeazzo, 154
Clark, General Mark, 63
Classification, Operation, 28
Clay, General Lucius D., 42, 134
Cohen, Kenneth, 39–40, 69
Collins, Michael, 60
Cominform: abolished, 144
Conant, James, 112, 154–5
'Conflict' *see* Smoky Joe's
Cookridge, E.H., 159
Counter-Intelligence Corps (CIC; US
  Army), 23
Crabb, Commander Lionel ('Buster'), 164,
  171, 173
Curiel, Henri, 70
Czechoslovakia: falls to Communists
  (1948), 19, 21

Dansey, Claude ('Colonel Z'), 23
Dasher, General Charles L., 152–3, 155
Dawson, Robert, 170
Dibrova, Major-General, 142
Distant Early Warning Line (DEW), USA-
  Canada, 89
Donovan, William ('Wild Bill'), 42
Doolittle, Lieutenant-General James,
  103–4
Dreier, Alex, 157
Dudakov, General, 150
Dulles, Allen: on Berlin tunnel, 2, 11;
  background, 11–12, 82, 84; portrayed,
  52; Rowlett assists, 53; Harvey reports
  to, 57; character and qualities, 82, 94;
  reviews and approves tunnel plan, 82–3,
  87, 98; employs US Army Corps of
  Engineers for tunnel building, 99–100;
  disputes with Joseph McCarthy, 104;
  authorized to proceed, 104; on finite life
  of Berlin tunnel, 110; and security of
  tunnel, 111–13; anxiety over Berlin, 145;
  on exposure of Berlin tunnel, 146, 148,
  165; Barnes works with, 154; briefs
  Selwyn Lloyd on U-2 operation, 173; on
  efficacy of U-2 plane, 174; Grose's
  biography of, 184, 189; requests
  information from Berlin tunnel, 187;
  The Craft of Intelligence, 182
Dulles, John Foster, 83, 89, 117, *118*
Durie, Willie, 186

Index

Ebert, Fritz, 166

'echo effect', 38, 40–1

Eden, Sir Anthony (*later* 1st Earl of Avon):
secrecy over British involvement in
Berlin tunnel, 12; in Carlton Gardens,
63; at Geneva summit (1955), 116; warns
against attack on Berlin, 145; and
Khrushchev-Bulganin visit to Britain,
161, *161*; accepts invitation to USSR,
163; declines to authorize second Berlin
tunnel, 171; bans U-2 flights from
Britain, 173; resigns, 174

Eisenhower, Dwight D.: elected President
(1952), 48, 59; Strong advises, 61; and
Allen Dulles, 82–3, 104; summit with
Churchill (Bermuda, 1953), 88, 91, 93;
demands intelligence on Soviet
intentions, 103; at 1955 Geneva summit,
116–17; warns against attack on West
Berlin, 145–6; and exposure of Berlin
tunnel, 165; and proposal for second
Berlin tunnel, 171; meeting with
Macmillan (Bermuda, 1957), 174

Elizabeth II, Queen: Coronation, 91;
Khrushchev and Bulganin meet, 162

Elliott, Nicholas, 39, 85

Evans, Joe, 124–6, 128, 132–3, 136, 147,
181–2

Faure, Edgar, 116

Federal Bureau of Investigation (FBI), 3

Fesq, Suzanne, 18

Field Security (British), 22, 31–2

'Fleetfoot' (agent), 57, 78, 84

Fleming, Ian, 7; *Casino Royale*, 91

Foreign Office (British): receives Vienna
intelligence, 65; and warnings of Soviet
attack, 90

Forster, John, 169

Forward Processing Unit (FPU), 96, 128

Frankfurter Allgemeine (newspaper), 167

Franks, Dicky, 175

'Fred' (CIA officer), 122, 124

Freisler, Roland, 88

Fuchs, Klaus, 39

Gablons (imitation jewellery firm), 34

Gaitskell, Hugh, 162

Gardner, Meredith, 48

Gehlen, General Reinhard: intelligence
organization, 158–9

Geneva: 1955 summit, 116–17

Germany: as centre of intelligence, 43;
division and reunification question, 88–9

Germany, East (German Democratic

Republic): Soviet forces in, 91, 136;
recognized by USSR, 131; status in
Berlin, 131–2; as source of uranium,
134; Soviet intelligence and counter-
intelligence in, 137; uprising (1953),
139; treaty with USSR (1955), 145; and
discovery of tunnel, 146; denounces
West Berlin as US and NATO spy base,
166–7; collapse, 184, 186

Germany, West (Federal Republic of
Germany): rearmament, 89; intelligence
organization (BND), 159

Gimson, Tom, 63, 65–6, 72–3, 91, 94, 96,
114

Gold, Operation *see* Stopwatch/Gold,
Operation

Goleniewski, Lieutenant-Colonel Michael
('Sniper'), 175

Goncharev, Vadim, 143–4

Goodpaster, Andrew, 165

Gorbachev, Mikhail, 179

Gordievsky, Oleg, 179

Government Communications
Headquarters (GCHQ; British): receives
items from Vienna cable-tapping, 30;
and Venona, 47; intelligence gathering,
60; and handling of Berlin tunnel
messages, 95, 124

Grechko, Marshal Andrei, 132–3, 141–4,
146, 182

Greene, Graham, 19–20, 35

Greer, Brigadier Eric, 122

Grivas, George, 27

Grose, Peter, 184, 186, 189

GRU (Soviet Military Intelligence): in
Vienna, 21

Haase, Major Werner, 158

Hanssen, Robert, 3

Hargrove, Charles, 160

Harrell, Major-General Ben, 107

Harvey, William (Bill) King: background
and character, 51–2, *52*; and plans for
Berlin tunnel, 53–4, 57, 78, 82; arrives
in Berlin, 77; relations with Lunn, 86;
and composition of processing units,
95–6; takes lease on Rudow land,
98–9; and construction of tunnel, 103,
105, 107; and safeguarding tunnel
security, 110–12; Montgomery liaises
with, 120; Murphy works with,
129–30; Popov supplies information to,
130; runs double agents, 137; and
Soviet discovery of tunnel, 147–54,
159, 162

Index

Helms, Richard: on Vienna, 19, 36; Rowlett reports to, 53; brings in SIS on Berlin tunnel plan, 83

Hersh, Burton: *The Old Boys*, 165

Hillgarth, Alan, 60–1

Hitler, Adolf: at 1936 Winter Games, 16; annexes Austria, 18; discussions with Oshima overheard, 50

Hobson, Valerie (Mrs John Profumo), 122

HOMER (information source), 39

Hood, William, 36, 139

Horne, Alistair, 88

Hungary: 1956 rising, 6, 132; under Soviet control, 21

Hunt, (Sir) John, 90

Hyde, Harford Montgomery, 115

hydrogen bomb: USA develops, 89; USSR tests, 103

Idris, King of Libya, 27

Illegal Frontier Crossers (IFCs; Austria), 22

Irvine, Andrew, 14

John, Otto, 11

Joint Intelligence Bureau (British), 61

Joint Intelligence Committee (British): and warnings on Soviet attack, 59, 90, 93, 104–5, 188; orders eavesdropping programme, 61; and US-British discrepancies on estimates of Soviet equipment, 110

Joint Services Intelligence Group for Germany, 92

Kalyagin, Lieutenant-General, 142

Karlshorst (KGB's Berlin HQ), 56–7, 130, 138, 147, 149–50, 155

Keitel, Field-Marshal Wilhelm, 7

Kennedy, John F.: assassination, 178

KGB: awareness of Berlin tunnel plan, 2, 143, 146; Special Bureau (Spetsburo) no. 1, 6; activities in Berlin, 7; kidnappings, 11; in Vienna, 21; recruits Blake, 70–2; in Manchuria, 71; learns of Vienna tunnel, 76; Blake passes information to, 97–8, 115, 143, 160, 183; taps US cable near Potsdam, 138, 143; plants false defectors, 142; exploits exposure of Berlin tunnel, 157–8, 160; and Gehlen organization, 159; protects Blake over secrecy of Berlin tunnel, 180–3, 188; collapses, 184

Khrushchev, Nikita S.: visits Britain, 12, 161–4, *161*, 173; at Geneva summit (1955), 116–17; on Soviet position in

Berlin, 131–2; denounces Stalin, 132–3, 135, 144–5, 188; reappoints Zhukov, 135–6; promises to reduce Soviet armed forces, 136; and exposure of Berlin tunnel, 144–6, 163; tough attitude towards West, 145–6; propaganda against West Germany, 159

Killian, James, 103

Kindell, F.E. (Eddie), 78

King, Andrew: in charge of Austrian operations, 23–4, 25; informs CIA of Vienna tunnel operation, 38; suspected, interrogated and cleared by Thistlethwaite, 39–40; recruits Blake for SIS, 69; in Berne with Dulles, 84; as deputy to Elliott, 85; oversees Chester Terrace operations, 122; urges revealing British involvement in Berlin tunnel, 169

Knightley, Philip: *The Second Oldest Profession*, 178

Kondrashev, Sergei Alexandrovich: controls Blake, 74–6, *75*, 96–8, 143, 179, 181–3, 186

Korda, Sir Alexander, 23

Korean War (1950–3): outbreak, 43, 48; prisoners return from, 67, 69–70; armistice, 90

Kotsiuba, Colonel Ivan, 10, 155, 157, 160, 173

Lamphere, Robert, 51–3, *52*

Le Carré, John (i.e. David Cornwell), 84

Le Tissier, Tony, 178

Lichleiter, Vyrl, 78, 93, 120

Lloyd, Selwyn (*later* Baron), 173

London Film Productions, 23

Longley-Cooke, Vice-Admiral Eric, 92–3

Lonsdale, Gordon (i.e. Konon Molody), 122

Lord, Operation, 35

Lumumba, Patrice, 53

Lunn, Sir Arnold, 16

Lunn, Sir Henry, 16

Lunn, Peter: background and character, 14, 15, 16–17; in Vienna, 14, 19–22, 24, 26, 31, 34, 41; joins SIS, 17; replaced by King, 24; supports Wyke, 27; keeps Vienna tunnel secret from CIA, 36–7; and Philby in Beirut, 39; provides intelligence to Churchill, 61; learns of Soviet intention not to attack, 65; in Berne, 84–5; post in Berlin, 84, 86, 94, 114–15; sets up technical section, 85; and composition of processing units, 95–6; urges continuing Berlin tunnel, 105; and safeguarding Berlin tunnel

Index